106 System Design Patterns for Interview Preparation

MOSTAFA GAMIL

CONTENTS

1: Introduction

1.1 What are system design patterns?

System design patterns are reusable solutions to common problems that arise in the design and implementation of software systems. These patterns provide a common language and a set of best practices for architects and developers to follow when designing and building large-scale software systems.

1.2 Why are system design patterns important?

In today's fast-paced and ever-changing technology landscape, system design patterns are more important than ever. They help architects and developers to make informed decisions about how to design and build systems that are scalable, resilient, and performant. Additionally, they provide a way to communicate design decisions and best practices to others in the organization.

1.3 Why is it important to know system design patterns before interviews?

Knowing system design patterns is essential for any software architect or developer looking to land a job at a top-tier company. Many major companies, such as the FAANG, are looking for candidates who have a deep understanding of these patterns and can apply them to real-world problems. This book provides a comprehensive overview of 106 different system design patterns and how they are used in the industry. Each pattern includes trade-offs, best practices, and real-world examples of usage from major companies and tools.

1.4 Who is this book for?

This book is for software architects and developers who are looking to improve their understanding of system design patterns, and for those who are preparing for technical interviews at top-tier companies. It is also useful for students and professionals who are interested in learning about the best practices and trade-offs for building large-scale software systems.

2: The 106 System Design Patterns

In this chapter, we will dive into 106 different system design patterns that are commonly used in the industry. These patterns cover a wide range of topics, including distributed systems, concurrency, caching, data storage, and security. The patterns are listed in alphabetical order, making it easy to find the specific pattern you are looking for. Each pattern includes a detailed explanation of how it works, trade-offs, best practices, and real-world examples of usage from major companies and tools. This comprehensive guide is an essential resource for anyone looking to improve their understanding of system design patterns and prepare for technical interviews at top-tier companies.

Active-Active

The "Active-Active" pattern is a system design pattern that allows for multiple instances of a service or system to be active and serve traffic simultaneously. This pattern is used to increase the availability and scalability of a system by allowing it to handle requests from multiple sources at the same time, rather than relying on a single instance or point of failure.

In an Active-Active system, multiple instances of a service or system are deployed and configured to work together, typically through a load balancer or other traffic management tool. Each instance is able to handle requests independently, and they are all able to read and write to the same shared data store, such as a database. This allows for a high degree of parallelism and fault tolerance, as requests can be handled by any available instance, and if one instance fails, others can continue to handle the traffic.

An example of a company that uses the Active-Active pattern is Google, they use this pattern in many of their services such as Google Search, Gmail, and Google Drive. Google uses various techniques like load balancing, data replication, and automatic failover to make this pattern work.

Trade-offs:

- This pattern can be complex to implement and requires careful planning and management to ensure data consistency is maintained across multiple instances.
- It can also increase the complexity of data management, as data needs to be consistently updated and synced across multiple instances

Best Practices:

- Use a load balancer or traffic management tool to distribute requests across multiple instances.
- Use a shared data store that supports replication and automatic failover.
- Monitor the system and instances to ensure that they are functioning as expected and that data consistency is maintained.

Real-world examples:

- Google's services such as Google Search, Gmail, and Google Drive use an Active-Active pattern to ensure high availability and scalability.

- Amazon's Elastic Load Balancer service supports active-active configurations.
- Microsoft Azure also supports active-active configurations through its Traffic Manager service.

API Gateway

The API Gateway pattern is a design pattern used to provide a single entry point for external consumers of a microservices-based system. It acts as a reverse proxy, routing incoming requests from clients to the appropriate service based on the request URL.

The API Gateway pattern can also provide additional functionality such as authentication, rate limiting, caching, and request/response transformation. This can help to improve the security, scalability, and maintainability of the system by offloading these responsibilities from the individual microservices.

API Gateway is often used in microservice architectures, where there may be many individual services that need to be exposed to external clients. Companies such as Amazon, Netflix, and Spotify have implemented the API Gateway pattern to improve the manageability of their microservices-based systems.

Trade-offs:

- It will add extra latency and complexity to the system as all requests have to pass through the API Gateway.
- It can become a bottleneck if not designed and scaled properly.

Best Practices:

- Implement caching and rate limiting in the API Gateway to reduce the load on the microservices.
- Use a reverse proxy such as Nginx or HAProxy for better performance.
- Use a cloud-based API Gateway service such as AWS API Gateway or Google Cloud Endpoints to offload the management of the Gateway.

Real-world examples:

- Amazon's API Gateway is a cloud-based service for creating and managing APIs for web and mobile applications.
- Netflix's Zuul is an open-source API Gateway that is used in the Netflix streaming service.
- Google Cloud Endpoints is a service that allows developers to create, deploy, and manage APIs on the Google Cloud Platform.

Ambassador

The Ambassador pattern is a variation of the API Gateway pattern, which is used to handle communication between microservices. The Ambassador pattern involves deploying a separate service, known as the Ambassador, that acts as a proxy or intermediary between the client and the microservices. The Ambassador is responsible for routing requests to the appropriate microservice, handling authentication and authorization, and providing other functionality such as caching, rate limiting, and monitoring.

One of the benefits of the Ambassador pattern is that it can help to decouple the client from the microservices, making it easier to change or update the microservices without affecting the client. Additionally, the Ambassador can provide a single point of entry for all requests to the microservices, simplifying security and monitoring.

Companies such as Datawire and Red Hat have open-sourced Ambassador, an implementation of the Ambassador pattern.

Trade-offs:

- It will add extra latency to the system as it will have to route the request through the Ambassador before reaching the microservice.
- It will add extra complexity to the system as it requires maintaining and configuring the Ambassador service.

Best Practices:

- Use a configurable and extensible Ambassador service.
- Monitor the Ambassador service for performance and errors.
- Use the Ambassador service for monitoring and logging, to centralize these concerns.
- Use the Ambassador service to provide security features, like rate limiting, authentication, and authorization.

Real-world examples:

- Ambassador is open-sourced by Datawire.
- Red Hat's 3scale API Management Platform includes an implementation of the Ambassador pattern.
- Istio, an open-source service mesh, includes support for the Ambassador pattern.

Anti-corruption Layer

Anti-Corruption Layer is a system design pattern that is used to protect a system from being affected by changes in external systems or data sources. It is a layer that sits between a system and an external data source and is responsible for converting or transforming the external data into a format that is understood by the system. This layer acts as a barrier that prevents any inconsistencies or invalid data from being propagated into the system.

The Anti-Corruption Layer is particularly useful in situations where a system needs to integrate with external systems or data sources that have different data structures, formats, or protocols. By providing a consistent and well-defined interface, the Anti-Corruption Layer makes it possible to integrate different systems and data sources in a seamless and robust way.

Trade-offs:

- it will add extra latency to the system as it will have to process the data before making a request.
- it will add extra memory usage to the system as it will have to keep track of the state of the external data.

Best Practices:

- Use a standard format for data exchange between the system and external data sources.

- The Anti-Corruption Layer should have minimal logic, and the majority of the logic should be in the external systems.

- Test the Anti-Corruption Layer separately to ensure that it is functioning correctly.

- Implement monitoring and logging to track the performance of the Anti-Corruption Layer.

Real-world examples:

- Many companies use Anti-Corruption Layer to integrate their internal systems with external data sources. For example, a company might use an Anti-Corruption Layer to convert data from a legacy system into a modern format that can be used by a newer system.

Asynchronous Request-Reply

The Asynchronous Request-Reply pattern is a way to handle requests and responses in an asynchronous manner, meaning that the request and response do not occur at the same time. Instead, the request is sent and the response is received at a later time. This pattern can be useful in situations where the response to a request may take a long time to be received, such as when the request is sent to a remote service or when the response is dependent on some external event.

In this pattern, the request is sent and a reply channel is provided for the response. The request sender can then continue with other tasks while waiting for the response to be received on the reply channel. When the response is received, it can be processed and the request sender can continue with any further processing.

This pattern can be implemented using message queues, where the request is sent to a queue and the response is received from a different queue. Companies such as Google and Microsoft use this pattern in their messaging systems to handle large numbers of requests and responses in an efficient manner.

Trade-offs:

- it can increase the complexity of the system as it requires adding and managing additional message queues.
- it can increase the latency of the system as the request and response are not happening in real-time.

Best Practices:

- Use a messaging system that supports message queues and asynchronous communication.
- Choose a messaging system that is reliable and can handle high loads.
- Monitor the message queues to ensure that they are not becoming overloaded.

Real-world examples:

- Apache Kafka is a distributed streaming platform that is commonly used to implement the Asynchronous Request-Reply pattern.
- RabbitMQ is a message broker that supports asynchronous communication and is commonly used to implement this pattern.

- Amazon SQS (Simple Queue Service) is a fully managed message queuing service that can be used to implement this pattern.

Backends for Frontends (BFF)

The Backends for Frontends (BFF) pattern is a microservices architectural pattern that is used to handle the needs of specific client applications. This pattern involves creating a separate backend service for each client application, or "frontend," that interacts with the main backend services of the system. This allows for a more flexible and modular design, as each client application can have its own unique set of requirements and constraints.

The BFF pattern can be used to address a number of challenges that arise when building microservice architectures. For example, it can be used to handle differences in security requirements, handle different types of data transformation, or to optimize communication between different services.

In the BFF pattern, the client application communicates with the BFF service, which acts as a proxy to the main backend services. The BFF service can handle tasks such as authentication, authorization, rate limiting, and data transformation. This allows the client application to interact with the backend services in a more efficient and secure way.

Companies such as Netflix and Uber have used the BFF pattern to improve the performance and scalability of their systems.

Trade-offs:

- The BFF pattern can increase the complexity of the system, as it requires additional services to be developed and maintained.
- It can also increase the number of network requests and data transfers, which can lead to latency issues.

Best Practices:

- Use the BFF pattern only when necessary.
- Keep the BFF service simple and focused on the needs of the specific client application.
- Monitor the performance of the BFF service to ensure that it is not becoming a bottleneck in the system.

Real-world examples:

- Netflix uses the BFF pattern to handle the unique requirements of different client applications, such as web and mobile applications.

- Uber uses the BFF pattern to optimize communication between their microservices and handle tasks such as rate limiting and data transformation.

Backpressure

Backpressure is a system design pattern used to handle high levels of incoming requests or data by slowing down the rate at which they are processed. This pattern helps prevent resource overload by controlling the flow of requests and data, ensuring that the system can handle incoming traffic without becoming overwhelmed.

The Backpressure pattern can be implemented in a number of ways, such as by using buffers or queues to store incoming requests and data, and controlling the rate at which they are processed. For example, a system might use a fixed-size buffer that only allows a certain number of requests to be processed at a time, and if the buffer is full, new requests are held in a queue until space becomes available.

Backpressure can be used in a variety of systems, such as distributed systems, networks, and streaming data systems. Companies such as Netflix and Twitter have implemented Backpressure to improve the performance and reliability of their systems.

Trade-offs:

- Backpressure can add latency to the system as it will have to hold requests in a queue until they can be processed.
- It can also add extra memory usage as it will have to keep track of the requests in the queue.

Best Practices:

- Monitor the system's resources to determine the appropriate buffer size and rate at which requests should be processed.
- Track metrics such as the number of requests in the queue, the rate at which requests are being processed, and the system's resource usage.
- Use a Backpressure library that supports configurable buffer sizes and rate controls.

Real-world examples:

- Reactor, a Java library for building asynchronous and reactive applications, includes support for backpressure.
- RxJava, a Java library for building reactive applications, also includes support for backpressure.

- Akka Streams, a library for building streaming data pipelines in Akka, includes support for backpressure.

Blackboard

The Blackboard pattern is a design pattern used to solve problems that involve multiple, concurrent, and cooperative processes. It is based on the idea of a central shared memory space, called a blackboard, where all processes can read and write data. The blackboard acts as a shared memory space where all the processes can share their knowledge and collaborate to solve a problem.

The blackboard pattern is typically used in AI and expert systems, where multiple processes work together to solve a problem. Each process is responsible for a specific aspect of the problem, and they all use the blackboard to share their knowledge and collaborate to find a solution.

One example of a company that uses the Blackboard pattern is IBM, which uses it in its Watson AI system. The Watson system uses a blackboard to store and share knowledge from multiple sources, such as databases, text, and speech, to find answers to questions.

Trade-offs:

- The Blackboard pattern can lead to complex interactions between processes, making it difficult to understand and debug the system.

- It can lead to contention and synchronization issues when multiple processes try to access the blackboard at the same time.

Best Practices:

- Define clear rules for how processes can interact with the blackboard to avoid contention and synchronization issues.
- Use a centralized logging system to monitor the interactions between processes and the blackboard.
- Use a robust and efficient data structure to implement the blackboard, such as a distributed hash table.

Real-world examples:

- IBM's Watson AI system uses a blackboard to store and share knowledge from multiple sources to find answers to questions.
- The blackboard pattern is also used in the RoboCup, a robot soccer competition, where multiple robots collaborate to play soccer using a shared blackboard.

Blue-Green Deployment

Blue-Green Deployment is a system design pattern used for releasing software updates with minimal downtime. The idea behind this pattern is to have two identical production environments, one called "blue" and the other called "green." The currently live environment is called "blue," and the new version of the software is deployed to "green." Once the new version of the software is fully tested and ready for release, the traffic is routed to the "green" environment, and the "blue" environment is put on standby. This way, if any issues arise with the new version of the software, the traffic can be quickly routed back to the "blue" environment, minimizing downtime.

This pattern is often used by companies such as Amazon, Netflix, and Facebook in order to minimize downtime during software releases and to allow for a rollback in case of issues.

Trade-offs:

- it requires having a duplicate environment ready at all times, which can be costly in terms of infrastructure and maintenance.
- it can be complex to set up and manage, especially in large and complex systems.

Best Practices:

- Ensure that the blue and green environments are identical and that all necessary configurations and dependencies are in place.

- Test the new version of the software thoroughly before releasing it to the green environment.

- Monitor the system during the release to quickly identify and address any issues that may arise.

- Perform a gradual rollout of the new version of the software to a small subset of users before releasing it to the entire user base.

Real-world examples:

- Amazon uses Blue-Green Deployment to release updates to its e-commerce platform with minimal downtime.

- Netflix uses Blue-Green Deployment to release updates to its streaming service with minimal downtime.

- Facebook uses Blue-Green Deployment to release updates to its social networking platform with minimal downtime.

Bulk Synchronous Parallel (BSP)

The Bulk Synchronous Parallel (BSP) pattern is a method of parallel computing that divides a large problem into smaller subproblems that are solved concurrently. The BSP pattern is based on the idea of dividing the computation into a sequence of supersteps, where each superstep is a combination of local computations and communication between the processors.

In a BSP system, each processor has a local memory and can perform computation and communication in parallel with other processors. The computation is divided into supersteps, where each superstep consists of a parallel computation phase followed by a global synchronization phase. In the parallel computation phase, each processor performs its local computation independently. In the global synchronization phase, all processors synchronize their state with each other before proceeding to the next superstep.

The BSP pattern is useful for solving large-scale problems that can be divided into smaller subproblems that can be solved concurrently. It is used in a variety of applications, including scientific computing, machine learning, and data analytics. Companies such as Google and IBM have used the BSP pattern to solve large-scale problems in their research and development projects.

Trade-offs:

- The BSP pattern requires a high degree of coordination between processors, which can add overhead and increase communication costs.
- The BSP pattern may not be well-suited for problems that have a high degree of data dependencies between subproblems.

Best Practices:

- Use a load-balancing strategy to evenly distribute the workload among processors.
- Use a fault-tolerance strategy to handle the failure of one or more processors.
- Use a performance monitoring and tuning tool to measure and optimize the performance of the BSP system.

Real-world examples:

- The Hadoop Distributed File System (HDFS) uses the BSP pattern to process large-scale data sets.

- The Apache Hama project is an open-source BSP framework for big data processing.
- The IBM Blue Gene supercomputer uses the BSP pattern to solve large-scale scientific and engineering problems.

Bulkhead

The Bulkhead pattern is used to isolate different parts of a system to prevent a failure in one part from spreading to the entire system. This is done by creating separate "compartments" or "bulkheads" within the system, each with its own resources and capacity.

When a failure occurs in one part of the system, it is contained within the bulkhead and does not affect the other parts of the system. This helps to maintain the overall availability and stability of the system.

The Bulkhead pattern can be used in various parts of a system such as thread pools, database connections, and network connections. It is commonly used in microservice architectures where different services are isolated to prevent a failure in one service from affecting the entire system.

Companies such as Netflix and Uber have implemented the Bulkhead pattern to improve the resiliency of their systems.

Trade-offs:

- it can add complexity to the system by introducing multiple bulkheads and managing them.

- it can also lead to increased resource usage as each bulkhead will have its own resources.

Best Practices:

- Use monitoring and alerting to detect failures and quickly isolate them to the appropriate bulkhead.
- Use appropriate tools such as thread pools and connection pools to implement bulkheads in different parts of the system.
- Regularly review the size and capacity of each bulkhead to ensure that it can handle the expected load.

Real-world examples:

- Netflix's Hystrix library includes support for implementing bulkheads in thread pools, database connections, and network connections.
- Istio, an open-source service mesh, includes support for implementing bulkheads in network connections through its Envoy proxy.

Cache-Aside

The Cache-Aside pattern is a technique used to efficiently manage the caching of data in a distributed system. This pattern involves keeping a copy of frequently accessed data in a cache, separate from the main storage, in order to improve performance.

When a request for data is made, the system first checks the cache for the requested data. If the data is found in the cache, it is returned to the caller. If the data is not found in the cache, it is retrieved from the main storage and added to the cache for future requests.

This pattern allows for faster access to frequently used data, as well as reduced load on the main storage. However, it also requires additional management of the cache, including eviction policies and cache invalidation.

Many companies, such as Netflix and Amazon, use the Cache-Aside pattern in their systems to improve performance and scalability. For example, Netflix uses this pattern in its content delivery system to cache frequently accessed movie and TV show data.

Trade-offs:

- It requires additional management of the cache, including eviction policies and cache invalidation.
- It can increase complexity and maintenance costs.
- It can lead to stale data if not handled properly.

Best Practices:

- Implement a cache eviction policy to remove stale data and make room for new data.
- Use a distributed cache to ensure high availability.
- Use a consistent hashing algorithm to distribute data across multiple cache nodes.
- Monitor the cache hit rate to ensure that the cache is being used effectively.

Real-world examples:

- Netflix uses the Cache-Aside pattern in its content delivery system to cache frequently accessed movie and TV show data.
- Amazon uses the Cache-Aside pattern in their retail website to cache product information and customer data.
- Many web applications and content management systems use this pattern to cache frequently accessed data such as web pages, images, and other static content.

Caching

Caching is a system design pattern that involves storing frequently accessed data in a temporary storage location (the cache) to reduce the number of times the data needs to be retrieved from the primary storage location. This can improve the performance of the system by reducing the latency of data access and reducing the load on the primary storage.

Caching can be implemented at various levels in a system, such as in-memory caching on the client side, caching in a load balancer, or caching on the server side. There are different caching strategies that can be used, such as Least Recently Used (LRU) or First In First Out (FIFO), and different cache eviction policies, such as time-based eviction or size-based eviction.

Caching can be used in many different types of systems, such as web applications, mobile apps, and microservices. Companies such as Netflix, Amazon, and Google use caching to improve the performance of their systems.

Trade-offs:

- Caching can add complexity to the system, as it requires managing the cache, such as invalidating stale data or dealing with cache eviction.

- Caching can also add additional memory usage to the system.

- Caching can also cause stale data if the data source is updated and the cache is not invalidated.

Best Practices:

- Use a caching library that supports configurable eviction policies and expiration times.

- Monitor the cache hit rate and adjust the cache size and eviction policy accordingly.

- Use a distributed cache to share cached data across multiple servers.

- Use a cache invalidation mechanism to ensure that stale data is not served.

Real-world examples:

- Memcached and Redis are popular open-source in-memory caching systems that can be used to cache data in web applications and microservices.

- Cloud providers such as AWS, Azure, and Google Cloud also offer managed caching services, such as ElastiCache and Cloud Memorystore.

Chaos Engineering

Chaos Engineering is the practice of intentionally introducing controlled failures or disruptions to a system in order to test its resilience and identify potential weaknesses. By simulating real-world failures, companies can proactively identify and fix issues before they occur in production. This pattern can be applied to various parts of a system such as network, storage, and application level.

Netflix is one company that has implemented Chaos Engineering in their system, using the tool Chaos Monkey to randomly shut down servers in their production environment. This helped them identify and fix potential issues before they could cause major problems.

Trade-offs:

- Introducing failures in the system can cause temporary service disruption
- It can be resource intensive to design and run controlled experiments

Best Practices:

- Start small and gradually increase the scope and complexity of experiments
- Have a clear rollback plan in case of unintended consequences
- Continuously monitor the system during and after experiments to ensure it returns to normal behavior
- Communicate with stakeholders about the experiments and their purpose

Real-world examples:

- Netflix's Chaos Monkey
- Gremlin's Chaos Engineering Platform
- AWS's Chaos Engineering for Amazon ECS and Amazon EKS.

It's worth noting that, Chaos Engineering is not a design pattern, it is a method of testing the robustness of a system by intentionally causing failures and monitoring how the system responds. It is a technique or approach that can be used in conjunction with other design patterns and best practices to improve the overall reliability and fault tolerance of a system.

Choreography

Choreography is a design pattern that allows for the coordination of multiple services in a distributed system without a central point of control. Instead, services communicate with each other through messages, and the coordination of the system emerges from the interactions between the services. This pattern is often used in microservices architectures and event-driven systems.

An example of choreography in action is a system that handles online purchases. The system may include several services, such as a catalog service, an inventory service, and a payment service. When a customer places an order, the catalog service sends a message to the inventory service to check the availability of the items. The inventory service then sends a message to the payment service to authorize the payment. Once the payment is authorized, the inventory service sends a message back to the catalog service to confirm the order and update the inventory.

The use of choreography in such a system allows for the different services to be developed and deployed independently, reducing the dependencies between them. However, it also requires a strong understanding of the interactions between services, and monitoring and testing the system can be more complex.

Companies such as Uber and Netflix have implemented choreography in their systems to enable the coordination of multiple services in a distributed system.

Trade-offs:

- Without a central point of control, it can be more difficult to understand the overall state of the system and to make changes to it.
- Choreography requires a strong understanding of the interactions between services and can be more complex to test and monitor.

Best practices:

- Use event-driven communication between services to facilitate choreography
- Use choreography in conjunction with other patterns such as Circuit Breaker to ensure the system remains stable and resilient.
- Use tools such as service meshes to monitor and control the interactions between services
- Ensure that services are loosely coupled and can be developed and deployed independently.

Real-world examples:

- Uber's architecture relies heavily on choreography to coordinate the interactions between the different services that make up the platform.
- Netflix's microservices architecture uses choreography to coordinate the interactions between the different services that make up the platform.
- Google's Istio service mesh includes support for choreography through its Envoy proxy.

Circuit Breaker

The Circuit Breaker pattern is used to handle failures in remote service calls by providing a mechanism to detect failures and temporarily stop requests to the failing service. This pattern can help prevent a cascade of failures in a distributed system by quickly identifying and isolating a failing service.

When a service call fails, the Circuit Breaker pattern counts the number of failures. If the number of failures exceeds a threshold within a specified time window, the Circuit Breaker trips and opens. Once the Circuit Breaker is open, it stops sending requests to the failing service. Instead, it returns an error to the caller, indicating that the service is unavailable.

After a period of time, the Circuit Breaker will attempt to close by sending a test request to the service. If the service is available and the test request is successful, the Circuit Breaker closes and resumes normal operation. If the service is still unavailable, the Circuit Breaker remains open and continues to return errors to the caller.

The Circuit Breaker pattern can be useful for systems that make a large number of remote service calls, such as microservice architectures. Companies such as Netflix and Netflix have implemented the Circuit Breaker pattern to improve the resiliency of their distributed systems.

Trade-offs:

- It will add extra latency to the system as it will have to check the state of the circuit breaker before making a request.
- It will add extra memory usage to the system as it will have to keep track of the state of the circuit breaker.

Best Practices:

- Start with a high threshold and low timeout values, and adjust them based on the specific needs of the system.
- Monitor the state of the Circuit Breaker to ensure that it is tripping and closing as expected.
- Track metrics such as the number of failures, the number of successful requests, and the number of requests that failed because the Circuit Breaker was open.
- Use a Circuit Breaker library that supports configurable timeouts and threshold values.

Real-world examples:

- Netflix's Hystrix library includes an implementation of the Circuit Breaker pattern.

- Spring Cloud Netflix includes support for the Circuit Breaker pattern through the Hystrix library.

- Istio, an open-source service mesh, includes support for the Circuit Breaker pattern through the Envoy proxy.

Circuit Breaker Proxy

The "Circuit Breaker Proxy" pattern is similar to the Circuit Breaker pattern, but instead of placing the Circuit Breaker logic directly in the service making the remote call, it is placed in a separate proxy service that sits in front of the service. The proxy service acts as a gatekeeper, monitoring the health of the service and directing traffic accordingly.

The Circuit Breaker Proxy pattern can be useful in situations where you have multiple services that need to make calls to a single, potentially unreliable service. By placing the Circuit Breaker logic in a separate proxy, you can avoid duplicating the logic in each service and centralize the management of the Circuit Breaker.

One real-world example of a company using the Circuit Breaker Proxy pattern is Amazon, which uses a service called AWS Elastic Load Balancer (ELB) as a proxy for its services. ELB can automatically detect when a service is unhealthy and route traffic away from it, protecting other services from cascading failures.

Trade-offs:

- It increases the complexity of the system by adding an extra layer between the services.

- It may introduce additional latency due to the need to route traffic through the proxy.

Best Practices:

- Monitor the state of the Circuit Breaker Proxy to ensure that it is functioning correctly.
- Use a Circuit Breaker Proxy library that supports configurable timeouts and threshold values.
- Consider using a service mesh, such as Istio, which includes built-in support for the Circuit Breaker Proxy pattern.

Real-world examples:

- Amazon Web Services Elastic Load Balancer (ELB) uses the Circuit Breaker Proxy pattern.
- Google Cloud Load Balancer (GCLB) also uses the Circuit Breaker Proxy pattern.
- Kubernetes Ingress, a Kubernetes resource, can be configured to act as a Circuit Breaker Proxy.

Circuit Breaker Toggling

The Circuit Breaker Toggling pattern is a variation of the Circuit Breaker pattern, in which the service calls are not completely stopped when the Circuit Breaker trips, but instead are reduced to a minimal level. This allows the system to continue to function while still protecting against cascading failures.

When a service call fails, the Circuit Breaker Toggling pattern counts the number of failures. If the number of failures exceeds a threshold within a specified time window, the Circuit Breaker trips and the rate of service calls is reduced by a certain percentage. Once the number of failures decreases and the service becomes available again, the rate of service calls is gradually increased back to normal.

This pattern can be useful for systems that need to maintain a certain level of availability, even in the face of failures. Companies such as Uber and Amazon have implemented the Circuit Breaker Toggling pattern to maintain a balance between availability and fault tolerance.

Trade-offs:

- It can add extra complexity to the system as it requires more monitoring and control over the service calls rate.

- It may lead to reduced system performance during failures.

Best Practices:

- Monitor the state of the Circuit Breaker and the rate of service calls.
- Implement a gradual increase in the rate of service calls to avoid overloading the service.

Real-world examples:

- Uber's service mesh, M3, includes an implementation of the Circuit Breaker Toggling pattern.
- Amazon's DynamoDB uses a similar pattern called Adaptive Capacity, which adjusts the rate of service calls based on the availability of the service.

Circuit Breaker with Fallback

This pattern is a variation of the Circuit Breaker pattern that also includes a fallback mechanism for handling failures.

When a service call fails, the Circuit Breaker pattern counts the number of failures. If the number of failures exceeds a threshold within a specified time window, the Circuit Breaker trips and opens. Once the Circuit Breaker is open, it stops sending requests to the failing service. Instead, it returns an error to the caller, indicating that the service is unavailable.

The Circuit Breaker with Fallback pattern adds an additional mechanism for handling failures. When a Circuit Breaker trips, instead of returning an error to the caller, the fallback mechanism is invoked. The fallback mechanism is a backup plan for handling the service call, such as using a cached version of the data or returning a default value. This allows the system to continue functioning even when a service call fails.

This pattern can be useful for systems that make a large number of remote service calls, such as microservice architectures. Companies such as Netflix and Spring Cloud have implemented the Circuit Breaker with Fallback pattern to improve the resiliency of their distributed systems.

Trade-offs:

- It will add extra latency to the system as it will have to check the state of the circuit breaker before making a request.

- It will add extra memory usage to the system as it will have to keep track of the state of the circuit breaker.

Best Practices:

- Start with a high threshold and low timeout values, and adjust them based on the specific needs of the system.

- Monitor the state of the Circuit Breaker to ensure that it is tripping and closing as expected.

- Track metrics such as the number of failures, the number of successful requests, and the number of requests that failed because the Circuit Breaker was open.

- Use a Circuit Breaker library that supports configurable timeouts and threshold values.

- Test the fallback mechanism to ensure that it can handle the expected failures.

Real-world examples:

- Netflix's Hystrix library includes an implementation of the Circuit Breaker with Fallback pattern.
- Spring Cloud Netflix includes support for the Circuit Breaker with Fallback pattern through the Hystrix library.
- Istio, an open source service mesh, includes support for the Circuit Breaker with Fallback pattern through the Envoy proxy.

Claim Check

The Claim Check pattern is a way to minimize the amount of data that needs to be transmitted or stored in memory during a process. Instead of sending or storing the entire data set, the Claim Check pattern sends or stores a smaller "claim check" token, which can be used to retrieve the original data at a later time.

The Claim Check pattern works by first storing the data set in a persistent storage system, such as a database or file system. Once the data is stored, a unique token is generated and sent back to the client. The client can then use this token to retrieve the original data from the storage system at a later time.

This pattern can be useful in systems where the data set is too large to be transmitted or stored in memory, or where the data needs to be stored for a long period of time. For example, an insurance company may use the Claim Check pattern to store large medical records, where a token is generated and sent to the patient, allowing them to retrieve the records at a later time.

Companies such as Amazon and Google have used the Claim Check pattern in their cloud storage systems, where users can upload large files and receive a token that can be used to retrieve the file at a later time.

Trade-offs:

- The claim check token can be lost or stolen, leading to data breaches.
- It increases latency as it requires additional steps to retrieve the original data.

Best Practices:

- Use a secure token generation mechanism to prevent unauthorized access to the data.
- Store the data in a highly available and durable storage system to ensure that it can be retrieved at any time.
- Monitor the claim check tokens to ensure that they are not being misused.

Real-world examples:

- Amazon S3 uses the Claim Check pattern to store large files, where a token is generated and sent to the user, allowing them to retrieve the file at a later time.

- Google Cloud Storage also uses the Claim Check pattern to store large files and provide a unique URL for users to download the data.

- Hadoop Distributed File System (HDFS) uses the Claim Check pattern, where data is stored in a distributed file system and a unique block ID is generated and sent to the client, allowing them to retrieve the data at a later time.

Client-side Discovery

The Client-side Discovery pattern is a way to handle service discovery in a distributed system. Instead of relying on a centralized service registry, clients are responsible for finding the location of a service they need to call. This can be done by sending a request to a well-known location, such as a load balancer or a DNS server, that returns the location of the service.

This pattern can be useful in situations where a centralized service registry is not possible or not desirable, such as in a large-scale distributed system with a high number of services or in a dynamic environment where services are frequently added or removed.

Companies such as Amazon and Netflix have implemented the Client-side Discovery pattern in their distributed systems to handle service discovery.

Trade-offs:

- It can add additional latency to requests as clients need to perform the service discovery before making a request.
- It can increase the complexity of the system as clients need to handle the discovery process.

Best Practices:

- Use a well-known location, such as a load balancer or a DNS server, for clients to perform service discovery.

- Cache the location of services to reduce the number of service discovery requests.

- Monitor the health of services and update the cached locations accordingly.

Real-world examples:

- Amazon's AWS service uses client-side discovery to handle service discovery for its EC2 instances.

- Netflix's Eureka service uses client-side discovery to handle service discovery for its microservices.

Client-side Load Balancing

Client-side Load Balancing is a pattern that allows for distributing client requests across multiple servers in a load-balanced manner. This pattern can be used to increase the overall capacity and reliability of a system by distributing the load across multiple servers. It is often used in combination with other patterns such as service discovery and circuit breaker to provide a robust and scalable architecture.

The pattern works by having the client maintain a list of available servers and using a load balancing algorithm to determine which server to send a request to. Common load balancing algorithms include round-robin, least connections, and IP hash. The client can also use service discovery to dynamically update its list of available servers.

An example of a company that uses this pattern is Netflix, which uses the Ribbon library for client-side load balancing in its microservice architecture.

Trade-offs:

- It can add complexity to the client as it needs to maintain a list of available servers and implement a load balancing algorithm.

- It can also add latency as the client needs to determine which server to send a request to before sending the request.

Best Practices:

- Use a load balancing algorithm that is appropriate for the specific needs of the system.
- Use service discovery to dynamically update the list of available servers.
- Monitor the load balancing to ensure that it is distributing the load as expected.
- Use a load balancing library that supports different algorithms and service discovery.

Real-world examples:

- Netflix's Ribbon library for client-side load balancing
- HAProxy, an open-source load balancer, can be used for client-side load balancing.
- Envoy, an open-source service mesh, also supports client-side load balancing.

Clock-Bound Wait

The Clock-Bound Wait pattern is used to handle delays in a distributed system by setting a maximum wait time for a response from a remote service. This pattern can help prevent a system from waiting indefinitely for a response from slow or unresponsive service, and instead, fail fast and take appropriate action.

The Clock-Bound Wait pattern works by setting a maximum wait time for a response from a remote service. Once the wait time has expired, the system will stop waiting for a response and take appropriate action, such as retrying the request, failing over to a backup service, or returning an error to the caller.

This pattern can be useful for systems that make a large number of remote service calls, such as microservice architectures. Companies such as Netflix and Amazon have implemented the Clock-Bound Wait pattern to improve the resiliency of their distributed systems.

Trade-offs:

- It will add extra latency to the system as it will have to wait for a fixed amount of time before taking any action.

- It will add extra memory usage to the system as it will have to keep track of the time.

Best Practices:

- Start with a high wait time, and adjust it based on the specific needs of the system.
- Monitor the wait times to ensure that they are within the expected range.
- Track metrics such as the number of successful requests, the number of requests that timed out, and the average wait time.
- Use a Clock-Bound Wait library that supports configurable wait times.

Real-world examples:

- Netflix's Hystrix library includes an implementation of the Clock-Bound Wait pattern.
- Spring Cloud Netflix includes support for the Clock-Bound Wait pattern through the Hystrix library.
- Istio, an open-source service mesh, includes support for the Clock-Bound Wait pattern through the Envoy proxy.

Compensating Transaction

The Compensating Transaction pattern is used to reverse the effects of a previously executed transaction in case of failure or error. This pattern can be used to ensure data consistency and integrity by undoing any changes made by a failed transaction and returning the system to its original state.

The pattern works by creating a "compensating transaction" that undoes the effects of the original transaction. This compensating transaction is typically executed when a failure or error is detected, and it is designed to restore the system to its original state before the failed transaction occurred.

The Compensating Transaction pattern can be used in a variety of systems, such as financial systems, inventory management systems, and e-commerce systems. Companies such as Amazon and PayPal use this pattern to ensure data consistency and integrity in their systems.

Trade-offs:

- It can add complexity to the system as it requires extra logic to handle the compensating transaction.
- It can add extra latency to the system as it may require additional time to execute the compensating transaction.

Best Practices:

- Design the compensating transaction to be as simple and efficient as possible.

- Test the compensating transaction thoroughly to ensure that it can undo the effects of the original transaction correctly.

- Monitor the system for failures and errors, and execute the compensating transaction as soon as a failure or error is detected.

- Keep a log of all transactions and their compensating transactions to aid in debugging and recovery.

Real-world examples:

- The AWS Lambda service uses the Compensating Transaction pattern to automatically roll back changes made by a failed Lambda function.

- The XA standard for distributed transactions, used by systems such as JTA and JTS, includes support for compensating transactions.

- The Saga pattern is a way to implement long-running transactions using a sequence of local transactions and compensating transactions.

Competing Consumers

The Competing Consumers pattern is a pattern used to handle concurrent access to a shared resource, such as a message queue or a database table. The pattern involves multiple consumers, or threads or processes, competing to retrieve and process the next available item in the shared resource.

The pattern is implemented by having each consumer repeatedly check the shared resource for new items, retrieve an item, and process it. When a consumer retrieves an item, it is typically marked as "in progress" or "locked" to prevent other consumers from processing the same item. Once the item is processed, it is marked as "complete" or "deleted" so that it is no longer available for processing.

The Competing Consumers pattern is commonly used in systems that process a large number of messages or tasks, such as message queues or task queues. Companies such as Twitter and LinkedIn have implemented the Competing Consumers pattern to improve the performance and scalability of their systems.

Trade-offs:

- It can lead to contention for shared resources, particularly when the rate of incoming items is high.

- It can lead to a high rate of polling the shared resource, which can have negative performance implications.

Best Practices:

- Implement a priority or fairness mechanism to ensure that items are processed in a fair and timely manner.
- Implement a back-off mechanism to reduce contention for shared resources.
- Monitor the rate of incoming items and the rate at which items are being processed to adjust the number of consumers as needed.
- Use a library or framework that supports the Competing Consumers pattern, such as Apache Kafka or RabbitMQ.

Real-world examples:

- Apache Kafka supports the Competing Consumers pattern through its consumer groups feature.
- RabbitMQ supports the Competing Consumers pattern through its consumer acknowledgment feature.
- AWS SQS supports the Competing Consumers pattern through its visibility timeout feature.

Compute Resource Consolidation

Compute Resource Consolidation is a system design pattern that aims to optimize the usage of compute resources in a distributed system. It involves consolidating multiple workloads onto a smaller number of physical or virtual machines to reduce costs and improve efficiency.

One way to achieve this is by using containerization technologies such as Docker or Kubernetes, which allow multiple workloads to run on a single host. Another approach is to use virtualization technologies like Hyper-V or VMware, which allow multiple virtual machines to run on a single physical host.

The Compute Resource Consolidation pattern can be used in a variety of systems, such as data centers, cloud environments, or edge computing systems. Companies such as Google and Amazon use this pattern to optimize the usage of resources in their data centers and cloud environments.

Trade-offs:

- Compute resource consolidation can lead to increased resource contention if not properly managed.

Best Practices:

- Monitor the resource usage of consolidated workloads to ensure that they do not interfere with each other
- Use container orchestration tools like Kubernetes to schedule and manage workloads on shared resources
- Use virtualization technologies like Hyper-V or VMware to run multiple virtual machines on a single physical host

Real-world examples:

- Google uses container orchestration with Kubernetes to optimize the usage of resources in its data centers.
- Amazon uses a combination of containerization and virtualization to optimize the usage of resources in its cloud environment.
- Docker uses containerization to allow multiple workloads to run on a single host, reducing resource usage and costs.

Command Query Responsibility Segregation (CQRS)

The Command Query Responsibility Segregation (CQRS) pattern is used to separate the responsibilities of handling commands, which change the state of a system, from handling queries, which return the current state of a system. This pattern can help to improve scalability and maintainability by allowing different parts of the system to handle different types of requests.

In a CQRS system, commands are sent to a Command Bus, which is responsible for handling the commands and updating the system's state. Queries are sent to a Query Bus, which is responsible for handling the queries and returning the current state of the system. The Command Bus and Query Bus can be implemented using different technologies, such as message queues or event streams, to handle the different types of requests.

The CQRS pattern can be useful for systems that have a high volume of read and write requests, such as e-commerce systems or financial systems. Companies such as Microsoft and EventStore have implemented the CQRS pattern to improve the scalability and maintainability of their systems.

Trade-offs:

- It increases the complexity of the system as different parts of the system will have to handle different types of requests.

- It requires more effort to maintain the system as the state of the system may be stored in different places.

Best Practices:

- Segregate the read and write models to separate the concerns.

- Use different data storage solutions for read and write models.

- Use a separate data model for read and write operations.

- Use different technologies for handling commands and queries.

- Use event sourcing to keep track of the changes in the system.

Real-world examples:

- EventStore, an open-source, event-sourced database, uses the CQRS pattern to handle commands and queries.

- Microsoft's Azure Service Bus supports the CQRS pattern by allowing developers to create separate queues for handling commands and queries.

Command-Query Separation (CQS)

The Command-Query Separation pattern is a design principle that states that every method or function should either perform an action or return information, but not both. In other words, it separates the responsibility of changing the state of the system (commands) from the responsibility of querying the state of the system (queries).

This pattern is commonly used in systems where multiple threads or processes are interacting with a shared state, as it helps to ensure that the state remains consistent and predictable. It also makes it easier to reason about the behavior of the system and to test individual components in isolation.

One example of a company that has used the Command-Query Separation pattern is Microsoft, which used it in the development of its Azure Service Fabric. The Service Fabric uses the pattern to separate the state management of services from the communication and coordination between services.

CQS can be used in combination with CQRS to provide more flexibility in the way the system is designed and implemented.

Trade-offs:

- It can increase the complexity of the codebase as it requires more methods and classes to be created.

Best Practices:

- Use clear naming conventions for commands and queries to make it easy to identify which methods perform actions and which return information.
- Use command and query objects to encapsulate the data and behavior of each operation.
- Use an in-memory event store to track the history of commands and events in the system.

Real-world examples:

- Microsoft Azure Service Fabric
- Greg Young's CQRS pattern
- Martin Fowler's Command-Query Separation pattern

Consistent Core

The Consistent Core pattern is a system design pattern that is used to ensure consistency in distributed systems. The pattern is based on the idea that a small, well-defined subset of the system, known as the "core", is responsible for maintaining consistency across all nodes in the system.

The core is responsible for handling all updates to the system's shared state, and it uses a set of rules and algorithms to ensure that all nodes in the system are in agreement about the current state of the system. The core also enforces constraints on the system's state, such as consistency and integrity, to ensure that the system remains in a valid state.

One example of this pattern is the Paxos algorithm, which is a distributed consensus algorithm that is used to ensure consistency in distributed systems. The Paxos algorithm uses a small subset of nodes, known as the "Paxos group", to ensure that all nodes in the system agree on the current state of the system. The Paxos group is responsible for handling updates to the system's shared state, and it uses a set of rules and algorithms to ensure that all nodes in the system are in agreement about the current state of the system.

Another example of this pattern is the use of consensus protocols in distributed databases such as Google's Spanner, which uses the Paxos algorithm to ensure consistency across all nodes in the system.

Trade-offs:

- The Consistent Core pattern can add extra complexity to the system as it requires a dedicated set of nodes to handle updates and maintain consistency across the system.
- It also adds extra latency to the system, as updates must be propagated to all nodes in the system before they can be considered complete.

Best Practices:

- Carefully design the core to minimize the number of nodes and minimize the number of rules and algorithms required to maintain consistency.
- Monitor the state of the core to ensure that it is maintaining consistency across all nodes in the system.
- Use a consensus algorithm that is well-suited for the specific needs of the system.

Real-world examples:

- Google's Spanner database uses the Paxos algorithm to ensure consistency across all nodes in the system.

- Apache ZooKeeper uses the Paxos algorithm to ensure consistency in its distributed coordination service.

- Ethereum blockchain uses the Practical Byzantine Fault Tolerance (PBFT) algorithm to ensure consistency across all nodes in the system.

Completeness Guarantee

Completeness guarantee is a system design pattern that ensures that all parts of a distributed system have a consistent and complete view of the system's state. This is typically achieved by implementing a consensus protocol such as Paxos or Raft, which ensures that all nodes in the system agree on the order of updates and that all updates are eventually applied to all nodes.

One key aspect of the completeness guarantee pattern is that it ensures that all updates are committed in the same order across all nodes in the system. This is important for maintaining consistency in distributed systems, as it ensures that all nodes have the same view of the system's state, even in the presence of network partitions or other failures.

Trade-offs:

- It increases the complexity of the system, as it requires implementing and maintaining a consensus protocol.
- It can also increase the latency of the system, as updates must be committed to all nodes before they can be considered complete.

Best practices:

- Monitor the performance of the consensus protocol to ensure that it is functioning correctly and that updates are being committed in a timely manner.
- Monitor the state of the system to ensure that all nodes have a consistent and complete view of the system's state.
- Implement a way to handle failures, such as a leader election process, in case a node goes down.

Real-world examples:

- Google's Spanner database uses Paxos to implement a completeness guarantee, allowing for strong consistency across all nodes in the system.
- Apache Kafka uses a replication protocol based on Raft to ensure that all nodes in a cluster have a consistent and complete view of the log.

Decision Tracking

Decision Tracking is a system design pattern that allows for the tracking and auditing of important decisions made by a system. It is particularly useful in systems that make automated decisions, such as in business processes or financial transactions.

The pattern involves capturing all relevant information about a decision, such as the decision criteria, inputs, and outcome, and storing it in a centralized decision repository. This repository can then be queried to view the history of decisions made by the system and to understand how and why a particular decision was made.

Decision tracking also allows for the implementation of decision governance, which is the process of managing and monitoring the decisions made by a system. This can include setting policies for decision-making, such as rules for compliance and ethical considerations, as well as monitoring the system's performance and taking corrective action if necessary.

Trade-offs:

- Decision tracking can add complexity to a system and increase the amount of data that needs to be stored and managed.

- It can also require additional resources for decision governance and monitoring.

Best Practices:

- Ensure that the decision repository is secure and only accessible to authorized personnel.
- Design the decision repository to be able to handle large amounts of data and be able to scale as the system grows.
- Ensure that the data stored in the decision repository is accurate and complete.
- Provide tools for easily querying the decision repository and analyzing the data stored in it.
- Implement decision governance policies and procedures to ensure compliance and ethical decision-making.

Real-world examples:

- In the financial industry, decision tracking is used to ensure compliance with regulations such as the Sarbanes-Oxley Act and the Dodd-Frank Wall Street Reform and Consumer Protection Act.
- In the healthcare industry, decision tracking is used to track clinical decision-making and ensure patient safety.

Deployment Stamps

Deployment Stamps is a system design pattern that allows for tracking the version and environment information of a deployed service or application. This pattern is often used in conjunction with continuous integration and continuous delivery (CI/CD) practices, where multiple versions of a service or application may be deployed to different environments (e.g. development, staging, production) at different times.

By including version and environment information as part of the deployment stamp, it becomes easier to track and identify which version of a service or application is currently running in a specific environment. This can be useful for troubleshooting issues, rollbacks, and for understanding the impact of a change in one environment on other environments.

Deployment stamps can be implemented by including version and environment information as part of the service or application's configuration, or by using a tool or library that automatically manages and attaches this information to the service or application. Examples of such tools are Spinnaker and Jenkins.

Trade-offs:

- It can increase the complexity of the system, as it requires maintaining version and environment information for each deployed service or application.

Best Practices:

- Automate the process of attaching deployment stamps to services or applications during the deployment process.
- Ensure that the deployment stamp information is easily accessible and understandable for troubleshooting and rollbacks.
- Use a consistent format for the deployment stamp information to make it easy to understand and use.

Real-world examples:

- Netflix uses the Deployment Stamps pattern to track versions of their services and applications.
- Google Cloud Platform uses the Deployment Stamps pattern to track versions of their services and applications.

Distributed Data

The Distributed Data pattern is a way of designing systems that can handle a large amount of data by distributing it across multiple machines. This is done by partitioning the data into smaller chunks, called shards, and storing each shard on a separate machine. This allows the system to scale horizontally, by adding more machines as the amount of data grows.

This pattern is often used in large-scale systems such as databases, search engines, and distributed file systems. Companies such as Google and Facebook use Distributed Data patterns to handle their large amount of data.

The key to implementing this pattern is to ensure that the data is distributed evenly across all the machines, and that each machine can handle the load of its assigned data. This is usually done by using a technique called sharding, where the data is partitioned based on a key, such as a hash of the data.

Another important aspect of the Distributed Data pattern is to ensure that the data is consistent across all machines. This is usually done by using a technique called replication, where each machine stores a copy of the data.

Trade-offs:

- The main trade-off of the Distributed Data pattern is the complexity it adds to the system. It can be difficult to ensure that the data is distributed evenly, and that it is consistent across all machines.

- Another trade-off is the added latency that comes with having to access data on multiple machines.

Best Practices:

- Use a sharding strategy that ensures data is distributed evenly across all machines.

- Use replication to ensure data consistency across all machines.

- Use load balancing to distribute incoming requests evenly across all machines.

- Monitor the system to ensure that the data is distributed evenly and that each machine is handling the load of its assigned data.

- Use a distributed data storage solution, such as a NoSQL database, to handle the complexity of a distributed data system.

Real-world examples:

- Google's Bigtable and Spanner databases use Distributed Data pattern to handle large amounts of data.

- Facebook's Cassandra and HBase databases use Distributed Data pattern to handle their large amounts of data.

- Amazon's DynamoDB and SimpleDB databases use Distributed Data pattern to handle large amounts of data.

Edge Workload Configuration

The Edge Workload Configuration pattern is a method of deploying and managing applications and services at the edge of a network, close to the source of data or the users who need it. The goal of this pattern is to reduce the latency and improve the responsiveness of the application by moving the processing closer to the data source or the users.

This pattern is commonly used in IoT, mobile and edge computing scenarios where data is generated at the edge and needs to be processed quickly before it is sent to the cloud or a data center. In these scenarios, edge devices such as gateways, routers, or other IoT devices are used to process the data and make decisions before sending it to the cloud.

For example, a company that uses IoT sensors to monitor the temperature and humidity in a warehouse could use the Edge Workload Configuration pattern to process the data from the sensors locally, and only send the data that exceeds certain thresholds to the cloud for further analysis. This reduces the amount of data sent to the cloud and improves the responsiveness of the system.

Some of the companies that use the Edge Workload Configuration pattern include Amazon Web Services, Microsoft Azure, and Google Cloud Platform. These companies offer edge computing services that allow customers to deploy applications and services at the edge of their network.

Trade-offs:

- It can be more expensive to deploy and maintain edge devices and services.
- It can be challenging to manage and monitor edge devices and services.
- It can be difficult to ensure data consistency and integrity when data is processed at the edge.

Best Practices:

- Identify the data that needs to be processed at the edge and the data that can be sent to the cloud or a data center.
- Use edge devices with sufficient processing power and storage capacity to handle the workload.
- Use a secure and reliable communication protocol to send data between the edge devices and the cloud or data center.

- Monitor the performance and availability of the edge devices and services.
- Regularly update and maintain the edge devices and services to ensure their security and reliability.

Real-world examples:

- Amazon Web Services Greengrass allows customers to run Lambda functions and communicate with IoT devices at the edge.
- Azure IoT Edge allows customers to run Azure services and custom code on IoT devices at the edge.
- Google Cloud IoT Edge allows customers to run Google Cloud services and custom code on IoT devices at the edge.

Emergent Leader

Emergent Leader is a system design pattern that is used to handle leader election in distributed systems. The pattern relies on a consensus algorithm to elect a leader among a group of nodes. The leader is responsible for coordinating the actions of the other nodes in the group.

The pattern works by having each node in the group continuously monitor the state of the other nodes in the group. If a node detects that the current leader is no longer responding or has failed, it will initiate a leader election process. During the leader election process, the nodes in the group will use the consensus algorithm to determine a new leader.

Once a new leader has been elected, it will take over the responsibilities of the previous leader and begin coordinating the actions of the other nodes in the group.

The Emergent Leader pattern can be useful for systems that require a leader to coordinate the actions of a group of nodes, such as distributed databases or distributed systems that rely on a leader to coordinate the actions of a group of workers.

Trade-offs:

- The pattern can add extra latency to the system as it requires nodes to continuously monitor the state of the other nodes in the group.
- It can also add extra complexity to the system as it requires the implementation of a consensus algorithm.

Best practices:

- Use a consensus algorithm that is well-suited for the specific needs of the system.
- Monitor the state of the leader to ensure that it is responding and coordinating the actions of the other nodes in the group.
- Track metrics such as the number of leader elections and the length of time it takes for a new leader to be elected.
- Use a library or framework that provides support for the Emergent Leader pattern.

Real-world examples:

- Apache ZooKeeper, an open-source distributed coordination service, uses the Emergent Leader pattern to handle leader election.

- The Raft consensus algorithm, which is used in distributed systems such as etcd and Consul, uses the Emergent Leader pattern to handle leader election.
- Apache Kafka, a distributed streaming platform, uses the Emergent Leader pattern to handle leader election for partitions.

Event Sourcing

Event Sourcing is a system design pattern that involves storing all changes to the state of an application as a sequence of events, rather than storing the current state directly. This approach allows for a complete record of the state changes over time, and can be useful for auditing, debugging, and rolling back to previous states.

In Event Sourcing, each event represents a single change to the state of the system, such as the creation of a new object or the modification of an existing one. These events are stored in a log, which can be used to rebuild the current state of the system. This log can be thought of as a history of all the changes that have occurred in the system.

One of the key benefits of Event Sourcing is that it allows for a more flexible and adaptable architecture. Because the events are stored separately from the current state of the system, it is easier to add new features and make changes without affecting the existing code. This can also help to improve scalability and performance.

Event Sourcing can be used in a variety of applications, including financial systems, e-commerce platforms, and gaming systems. Companies such as Microsoft, Intuit, and Zalando have used

Event Sourcing to improve the scalability and fault-tolerance of their systems.

Trade-offs:

- Event sourcing can make the system more complex and harder to understand, especially for developers who are not familiar with the pattern.
- It can also require more storage space to keep all the events, which can be costly.

Best Practices:

- Keep events simple and atomic to minimize complexity
- Keep the events stream in chronological order
- Store events in an append-only manner
- Use a separate tool to store and retrieve events

Real-world examples:

- Event Store is a database that implements Event Sourcing as its core feature.
- Apache Kafka is a distributed streaming platform that can be used to implement Event Sourcing.

- Event Sourcing is used in the Akka framework for building concurrent and distributed systems.

Explicit Public Events

Explicit Public Events is a design pattern that involves making certain events in a system explicitly public. This means that these events are explicitly defined and made available for other parts of the system to consume or react to.

This pattern is often used in event-driven architectures, where different parts of the system need to be notified of changes or updates in other parts of the system. By making these events explicit and public, it becomes easier to understand the interactions between different parts of the system and how they are affected by changes.

One example of using this pattern is in a retail e-commerce system, where a "product added to cart" event is made explicit and public. This event can then be consumed by other parts of the system, such as the inventory management system or the order processing system, to update their respective states.

Another example is in a social media application, where a "post liked" event is made explicit and public. This event can then be consumed by other parts of the system, such as the user's activity feed or the notifications system, to update their respective states.

Trade-offs:

- This pattern can add additional complexity to the system as it requires explicit definition and management of public events.
- It can also increase the number of dependencies between different parts of the system, making it more difficult to change or modify one part without affecting others.

Best Practices:

- Clearly define and document the public events in the system
- Use a consistent naming convention for events
- Use a publish-subscribe pattern for event delivery
- Limit the number of public events to only those that are necessary for the system's functionality
- Use a event management library or framework to handle event delivery and management.

Real-world examples:

- Apache Kafka, an open-source event streaming platform, uses the explicit public events pattern for handling event delivery and management.
- AWS SNS (Simple Notification Service) and SQS (Simple Queue Service) are services that allow for explicit public

events to be published and consumed in a decoupled manner.

External Configuration Store

The External Configuration Store pattern is a system design pattern that separates the configuration of a system from the code that uses it. This allows for easier management and updating of configuration without requiring changes to the codebase.

The pattern involves storing configuration data in an external store, such as a database or file system, and providing access to that store through a dedicated service or API. The system then retrieves the configuration data from the store at runtime and uses it to configure the system's behavior.

One benefit of this pattern is that it allows for dynamic updates to the system's behavior without requiring a code deployment. For example, a company could update a configuration setting in the external store to change the behavior of a system without having to deploy new code.

Another benefit is that it allows for different environments, such as development, staging, and production, to use different configurations without requiring different code deployments.

Companies such as Netflix and Airbnb have implemented the External Configuration Store pattern in their systems to improve manageability and scalability.

Trade-offs:

- It increases the complexity of the system as it needs to access the external store to retrieve configuration.
- It increases the latency of the system as it needs to access the external store to retrieve configuration.

Best Practices:

- Use a centralized configuration management tool to store and manage the configuration data.
- Use a version control system to track changes to the configuration data.
- Use a dedicated service or API to provide access to the configuration data.

Real-world examples:

- Netflix's Archaius library provides support for the External Configuration Store pattern.
- Spring Cloud Config provides support for the External Configuration Store pattern.
- HashiCorp's Vault can be used as an external configuration store for securing and managing sensitive configuration data.

Federated Architecture

The Federated Architecture pattern is used to create a loosely coupled system by allowing different components to work together without a central point of control. Instead of having a central point of control, each component of the system is able to operate independently and communicate with other components through a set of well-defined interfaces. This allows for a more flexible and adaptable system, as components can be added, removed, or replaced without affecting the overall system.

Federated Architecture is commonly used in systems that need to handle a large number of requests and handle them in a distributed way. This pattern is particularly useful for systems that need to scale horizontally and handle a large number of requests. Companies such as Amazon and Google use Federated Architecture to handle a large number of requests and handle them in a distributed way.

Trade-offs:

- Increased complexity due to the absence of a central point of control.
- More difficult to coordinate and manage when compared to monolithic architectures.

- Increased latency due to the need to communicate between different components.

Best Practices:

- Use well-defined interfaces to communicate between different components.
- Use a service discovery mechanism to locate and communicate with other components.
- Use load balancers to distribute the load between different components.
- Monitor the system to ensure that it is functioning as expected.

Real-world examples:

- Amazon's AWS is built on a Federated Architecture pattern.
- Google's GCP is also built on a Federated Architecture pattern.
- Kubernetes, an open-source container orchestration system, uses Federated Architecture to manage containers and services.

Federated Identity Management

The Federated Identity Management pattern typically uses a single sign-on (SSO) service that acts as a central point of authentication for all systems. This SSO service is responsible for authenticating users and providing a token or other form of identification that can be used by other systems to authenticate the user. The SSO service also manages the mapping of user identities across different systems, allowing for a single user to have different identities within different systems.

One example of a company that uses the Federated Identity Management pattern is Google, which allows users to use their Google account to sign in to other systems and websites. The Google SSO service authenticates the user and provides a token that can be used by the other systems to authenticate the user. This allows for a seamless user experience and centralized management of user identities.

Trade-offs:

- It can add complexity to the system, as it requires maintaining a central identity management service and integrating it with other systems.

- It can also add some latency and increase the number of requests needed to authenticate a user.

Best Practices:

- Use a robust and secure protocol for exchanging identity information, such as OAuth or OpenID Connect.
- Use encryption and secure communication methods to protect user identities and tokens.
- Use a centralized logging and monitoring system to keep track of user authentications and detect any suspicious activity.
- Regularly review and update the security and access controls of the SSO service.

Real-world examples:

- Google's SSO service is used to authenticate users across Google's various products and services, as well as to provide a SSO experience for non-Google websites and applications.
- Microsoft's Active Directory Federated Services (ADFS) is used to provide SSO and identity management for Microsoft's products and services, as well as for non-Microsoft systems.

- Okta is a popular SSO service that can be used to authenticate users across multiple systems and domains.

Failover

The Failover pattern provides a way to automatically redirect client requests to a backup service or server in the event of a failure or malfunction of the primary service or server. This pattern helps to ensure that the system remains available and responsive, even in the face of failures or other disruptions.

The Failover pattern is implemented by having multiple instances of a service or server running in parallel, with each instance monitored for health and availability. If the primary service or server becomes unavailable, client requests are automatically redirected to a backup service or server. The failover process can be triggered by a variety of conditions, such as a loss of network connectivity, a high error rate, or a failure to respond to health checks.

The Failover pattern is often used in high-availability systems and can be found in different domains such as databases, load balancers, and application servers. Companies such as Amazon, Microsoft, and Google Cloud Platform provide built-in failover mechanisms for their services.

Trade-offs:

- Additional cost for running multiple instances of the service or server.
- Additional complexity in configuring and managing the failover process.

Best Practices:

- Use automatic failover mechanisms to minimize the risk of human error.
- Monitor the health and availability of all service or server instances to detect failures quickly.
- Test failover scenarios regularly to ensure that the system is working as expected.
- Use load balancers to distribute traffic among multiple service or server instances for better performance.

Real-world examples:

- Amazon RDS provides automatic failover for its relational databases.
- Microsoft Azure provides automatic failover for its virtual machines.
- Google Cloud SQL provides automatic failover for its SQL databases.

Fault Tolerance

Fault tolerance is a system design pattern that aims to ensure the continued operation of a system despite the occurrence of faults or errors. This can be achieved through various techniques such as redundancy, replication, and error detection and recovery.

One common approach to achieving fault tolerance is through the use of redundancy, where multiple copies of a system or component are maintained in order to ensure that there is always a backup available in case of failure. For example, a load balancer can be used to distribute traffic across multiple servers, so that if one server fails, the load balancer can redirect traffic to the remaining servers.

Another approach is replication, where data is replicated across multiple nodes in a distributed system to ensure that the data is always available. This can be achieved through techniques such as master-slave replication or peer-to-peer replication.

Error detection and recovery is another key aspect of fault tolerance, where the system is designed to detect errors and take appropriate action to recover from them. This can be achieved through techniques such as health monitoring, failover, and self-healing systems.

Companies such as Google and Amazon use fault tolerance techniques in their systems to ensure high availability and reliability. For example, Google's Spanner uses a combination of atomic clocks and Paxos algorithm for distributed consensus to achieve high reliability and low latency. Amazon's DynamoDB uses a combination of consistent hashing, replication, and quorum-based protocols to ensure high availability and fault tolerance.

Trade-offs:

- Adding fault tolerance to a system can increase complexity and cost. It also adds latency to the system as the system needs to check for faults and perform recovery actions.

Best Practices:

- Use redundancy and replication to ensure that there is always a backup available in case of failure
- Use health monitoring and failover to detect and recover from errors
- Use self-healing systems to automatically repair failures
- Regularly test and monitor the system to ensure that it is functioning correctly

- Keep the system simple, so that it is easier to understand and maintain.

Real-world examples:

- Google's Spanner
- Amazon's DynamoDB
- Netflix's Chaos Monkey
- AWS Elastic Block Storage (EBS)
- Kubernetes and other container orchestration systems

Fixed Partitions

The Fixed Partitions pattern is used to distribute data across multiple nodes in a distributed system. This pattern involves dividing the data set into a fixed number of partitions and assigning each partition to a specific node in the system. This allows for efficient data distribution and improves the scalability of the system.

This pattern is often used in databases, where data is partitioned based on a specific key and each partition is assigned to a specific node. This allows for efficient data retrieval and improves the performance of the system.

Companies such as Google and Amazon use the Fixed Partitions pattern in their distributed databases to improve scalability and performance.

Trade-offs:

- The number of partitions must be determined in advance and cannot be easily changed, making it difficult to adapt to changes in the data set or system.
- The partitioning key must be chosen carefully to ensure an even distribution of data across the nodes, otherwise, some

nodes may become overloaded while others are underutilized.

Best Practices:

- Use a consistent hashing algorithm to determine which partition a piece of data belongs to, this ensures that data is distributed evenly across the nodes
- Monitor the load on each node to ensure that the data is being distributed evenly
- Use a partitioning key that has a good distribution of values to ensure an even distribution of data across the nodes

Real-world examples:

- Google's Bigtable and Amazon's DynamoDB use the Fixed Partitions pattern to distribute data across multiple nodes
- Apache Cassandra and MongoDB also use the Fixed Partitions pattern to distribute data across multiple nodes in a distributed system.

Follower Reads

Follower Reads is a system design pattern that is used to increase the scalability and performance of read operations in a distributed system. In this pattern, a master node is responsible for handling all write operations, while multiple follower nodes handle read operations. The follower nodes are typically read-only replicas of the master node, and they are updated with the latest data through replication.

This pattern allows the system to handle a large number of read requests by distributing them among the follower nodes. This reduces the load on the master node and increases the overall performance of the system. Additionally, it also allows the system to serve read requests even if the master node is unavailable, as the follower nodes can continue to serve requests.

Follower Reads can be used in a variety of systems, such as databases, caches, and search engines. Companies such as Twitter, LinkedIn, and Facebook have implemented this pattern to improve the scalability and performance of their systems.

Trade-offs:

- The replication process can add some latency to the system, as the follower nodes need to be updated with the latest data from the master node
- The system becomes more complex as it now needs to handle replication and synchronization between the master and follower nodes
- There is a risk of data consistency issues if the replication process is not implemented correctly

Best Practices:

- Use a replication protocol that is designed for high-performance and low-latency, such as log-based replication
- Monitor the replication process to ensure that the follower nodes are always in sync with the master node
- Use a load balancer to distribute read requests among the follower nodes
- Use a consistent hashing algorithm to map keys to nodes in order to minimize the number of key migrations
- Implement monitoring and alerting to detect and diagnose replication issues

Real-world examples:

- MySQL uses a master-slave replication model, where the master node handles write operations and the slave nodes handle read operations

- MongoDB uses a replica set, where one node acts as the primary and handles write operations, while the other nodes act as secondaries and handle read operations

- Cassandra uses a peer-to-peer replication model, where all nodes can handle both read and write operations, but some nodes are designated as replica nodes to handle read operations.

Generation Clock

The Generation Clock pattern is a technique used to maintain a consistent order of events across a distributed system. It is often used in systems that require a global order of events, such as distributed databases or distributed systems that need to implement a consensus algorithm.

The Generation Clock pattern works by assigning a unique timestamp, or generation, to each event that occurs in the system. The generation is incremented with each new event, ensuring that each event has a unique and increasing timestamp. This timestamp is used to order the events, so that all systems in the distributed system can agree on the order in which events occurred.

The Generation Clock pattern is used to solve the problem of maintaining a consistent global order of events in a distributed system, where the clocks of different systems may not be perfectly synchronized. This pattern is often used in distributed databases and distributed systems that need to implement a consensus algorithm, such as Paxos or Raft.

Companies such as Google and Amazon have implemented the Generation Clock pattern in their distributed systems to maintain a consistent order of events.

Trade-offs:

- The Generation Clock pattern can add extra overhead to a distributed system as it requires maintaining and updating the generation timestamp for each event.
- It can also add complexity to the system as it requires coordination between different systems to maintain a consistent global order of events.

Best Practices:

- Use a monotonic clock to generate timestamps, to avoid issues with clock drift.
- Use a unique identifier for each event in addition to the generation timestamp to ensure that events can be properly ordered even in cases where the generation timestamps are the same.
- Monitor the system to ensure that the timestamps are being generated and updated correctly.

Real-world examples:

- Google's Spanner distributed database uses the Generation Clock pattern to maintain a consistent global order of events.

- Amazon's DynamoDB uses the Generation Clock pattern to maintain a consistent order of events in their distributed key-value store.

- It is a technique used to maintain a consistent order of events across a distributed system. It is often used in systems that require a global order of events, such as distributed databases or distributed systems that need to implement a consensus algorithm.

Gatekeeper

The Gatekeeper pattern is a system design pattern that is used to control access to a resource or service by enforcing security and compliance policies. It acts as a gate that verifies and authenticates incoming requests before they are allowed to access the resource or service.

The Gatekeeper pattern is commonly used in microservice architectures, where different services may have different security and compliance requirements. By implementing a Gatekeeper at the entry point of each service, it is possible to enforce these requirements consistently across the entire system.

For example, a company may use a Gatekeeper pattern to ensure that all requests to access sensitive customer data are authenticated and authorized before being allowed to access the data. The Gatekeeper would check the incoming request for a valid authentication token and then check the authorization of the user making the request against the company's security policies.

Trade-offs:

- It will add extra latency to the system as it will have to check the state of the gatekeeper before making a request.

- It will add extra memory usage to the system as it will have to keep track of the state of the gatekeeper.

Best Practices:

- Use a standard authentication and authorization protocol, such as OAuth or OpenID Connect, to ensure compatibility with other systems.
- Monitor the state of the Gatekeeper to ensure that it is functioning as expected.
- Track metrics such as the number of successful and denied requests to help identify potential security issues.

Real-world examples:

- Netflix's Zuul is a popular open-source implementation of the Gatekeeper pattern.
- Istio, an open-source service mesh, includes support for the Gatekeeper pattern through its Envoy proxy.
- AWS API Gateway and Azure API Management are examples of cloud-based gatekeepers.

Gateway Aggregator

The Gateway Aggregator pattern is used to aggregating multiple service calls into a single request to improve performance and reduce latency. Instead of making separate requests to each service, the Gateway Aggregator makes a single request to a gateway that then forwards the request to the appropriate services and collects the responses.

This pattern is typically used in microservice architectures where there are many small services that need to be called to complete a single task. By aggregating the service calls, the Gateway Aggregator reduces the number of network trips and improves the overall performance of the system.

For example, in an e-commerce system, a customer may want to view their order history. Instead of making separate requests to the customer service, the order service, and the shipping service, the Gateway Aggregator can make a single request to a gateway that then forwards the request to the appropriate services and collects the responses.

The Gateway Aggregator pattern can also improve the scalability of the system, as it reduces the number of requests that need to be handled by each service. However, it also increases the complexity of the system and can make it more difficult to troubleshoot and maintain.

Some companies that use the Gateway Aggregator pattern include Amazon and Netflix. They use it to aggregate multiple service calls into a single request to improve performance and reduce latency.

Trade-offs:

- It can increase the complexity of the system
- It can make it more difficult to troubleshoot and maintain

Best Practices:

- Use caching to reduce the number of requests to the services
- Design the Gateway Aggregator to be stateless
- Monitor the Gateway Aggregator to ensure that it is working as expected

Real-world examples:

- Amazon's API Gateway uses the Gateway Aggregator pattern to aggregate multiple service calls into a single request to improve performance and reduce latency.

- Netflix's Zuul is an open-source API Gateway that uses the Gateway Aggregator pattern.

Gateway Offloading

Gateway Offloading is a system design pattern that is used to move certain processing tasks from the core services or applications to a separate gateway component. This can help to reduce the load on the core services and improve their performance. The gateway component can handle tasks such as authentication, authorization, rate-limiting, caching, and other types of processing that are not directly related to the core business logic of the system.

An example of this pattern in use is an e-commerce platform that uses a gateway to handle authentication and authorization for all incoming requests. The gateway is responsible for checking the user's credentials and ensuring they have the necessary permissions to access the requested resources. This allows the core services to focus on processing the business logic and fulfilling the user's requests, rather than spending resources on authentication and authorization.

Companies such as Amazon and Netflix have implemented the Gateway Offloading pattern to improve the performance and scalability of their systems.

Trade-offs:

- It may add complexity to the system as it introduces a new component that needs to be developed, deployed, and maintained.

- It may add some latency to the system as the request needs to go through the gateway before it reaches the core services.

Best Practices:

- Keep the gateway component as simple as possible, only include the necessary functionality.

- Monitor the gateway's performance and capacity to ensure that it can handle the load.

- Use a Gateway Offloading library that supports configurable functionality and can be easily integrated with the existing system.

- Use a protocol and data format that is efficient and easy to use.

Real-world examples:

- Amazon Web Services API Gateway
- Netflix Zuul
- Spring Cloud Gateway
- Express Gateway

- Kong API Gateway

Gateway Routing

The Gateway Routing pattern is a system design pattern used to route incoming requests to the appropriate service or backend. This pattern can be used in microservice architectures or other distributed systems to ensure that requests are handled by the appropriate service and to provide a single point of entry for incoming requests.

The Gateway Routing pattern typically involves using a reverse proxy or API gateway that sits in front of the service or backend. This gateway is responsible for routing incoming requests to the appropriate service or backend based on the URL or other request information. The gateway may also perform other functions such as authentication, rate limiting, and request/response transformation.

The Gateway Routing pattern can be useful for systems that have multiple services or backends that need to handle different types of requests. Companies such as Netflix and Amazon have implemented the Gateway Routing pattern to improve the scalability and security of their microservice architectures.

Trade-offs:

- It can add an extra layer of complexity to the system as the routing needs to be configured and managed.
- It can add extra latency to the system as requests have to pass through the gateway before reaching the appropriate service or backend.

Best Practices:

- Use a reverse proxy or API gateway that can handle high traffic and scale horizontally.
- Configure the gateway to route requests to the appropriate service or backend based on the URL or other request information.
- Use the gateway to perform functions such as authentication, rate limiting, and request/response transformation.
- Monitor the gateway to ensure that it is routing requests to the appropriate service or backend.

Real-world examples:

- Netflix's Zuul API gateway uses the Gateway Routing pattern.
- Amazon's API Gateway uses the Gateway Routing pattern.

- NGINX is an open-source web server and reverse proxy that can be used to implement the Gateway Routing pattern.

Gossip Dissemination

Gossip Dissemination is a system design pattern used for distributed systems to share information and updates between nodes in a network. It is based on the idea of nodes sharing information with each other in a peer-to-peer fashion, rather than through a centralized authority.

The Gossip Dissemination pattern works by having each node in the network maintain a set of information about other nodes in the network. Periodically, each node will select a random subset of nodes to share its information with. These selected nodes will then in turn share the information with their own set of nodes, and so on. This process continues until all nodes in the network have received the information.

One of the key benefits of the Gossip Dissemination pattern is that it can handle network partitions and node failures. If a node goes down, its information will eventually be disseminated to the rest of the network through the gossip process. Additionally, because the dissemination is done through a random subset of nodes, the pattern can handle large networks with thousands of nodes.

Trade-offs:

- It can add additional network traffic and CPU usage as nodes share information with each other.
- It can be difficult to determine the accuracy of information as it's disseminated through the network.
- It may take some time for new information to be disseminated throughout the entire network.

Best Practices:

- Use a Gossip Dissemination library that supports configurable intervals for disseminating information.
- Keep the information shared through Gossip Dissemination to a minimum to reduce network traffic and CPU usage.
- Use a mechanism for determining the accuracy of information shared through Gossip Dissemination.

Real-world examples:

- Apache Cassandra, a distributed NoSQL database, uses the Gossip Dissemination pattern for node communication and failure detection.
- The Akka actor model for concurrent programming, uses Gossip Dissemination for cluster membership and failure detection.

- The Hashicorp Serf tool, uses Gossip Dissemination for cluster membership and failure detection.

Health Check

The Health Check pattern is a system design pattern that allows a system to periodically check the health of its components and take appropriate action if a component is found to be unhealthy. The health check can be used to detect and recover from failures, or to proactively take preventative measures to avoid failures.

The Health Check pattern typically involves a central service that periodically sends health check requests to each of the system's components. The components are responsible for responding to these requests with their current health status. The central service then evaluates the responses and takes appropriate action based on the health status of the components.

This pattern can be used in a variety of systems, such as distributed systems, microservice architectures, and containerized environments. Companies such as Google and Amazon have implemented the Health Check pattern to improve the availability and reliability of their systems.

Trade-offs:

- The Health Check pattern can add overhead to the system as it requires additional resources to periodically check the health of components.

- The Health Check pattern can also add complexity to the system as it requires coordinating the health check requests and responses between the central service and the components.

Best Practices:

- Define clear and consistent criteria for determining the health of a component
- Use a centralized service for coordinating the health check requests and responses
- Monitor the health check results to identify and diagnose issues
- Use a Health Check library that supports configurable check intervals and threshold values.

Real-world examples:

- Kubernetes, an open-source container orchestration system, includes support for the Health Check pattern through the Kubernetes API and kubectl command-line tool.
- Docker, an open-source platform for developing, shipping, and running applications, includes support for the Health

Check pattern through the HEALTHCHECK instruction in the Dockerfile.

- AWS Elastic Load Balancing (ELB) supports the Health Check pattern by periodically sending HTTP or TCP requests to the registered instances and only routing traffic to instances that pass the health check.

High-Water Mark

The High-Water Mark pattern is a technique used in distributed systems to track the progress of a process or operation. It is used to ensure that data is not lost or duplicated in the event of a failure. The pattern uses a marker, called the "high-water mark," to indicate the point in the process or operation up to which data has been successfully processed. If a failure occurs, the system can use the high-water mark to determine which data needs to be processed again and which data has already been successfully processed and can be ignored.

The High-Water Mark pattern is often used in systems that process large amounts of data, such as data warehousing or big data systems. For example, in a data warehousing system, the High-Water Mark pattern can be used to track the progress of a data loading process. If a failure occurs during the loading process, the system can use the high-water mark to determine which data needs to be loaded again and which data has already been loaded and can be ignored.

Trade-offs:

- It can add extra complexity to the system as it needs to maintain the state of high-water mark

- It can add extra latency to the system as it needs to check the state of high-water mark before processing each data

Best Practices:

- Use a durable storage for the high-water mark state, such as a database or a message queue, to ensure that it can survive system failures
- Monitor the state of the high-water mark to ensure that it is being updated as expected
- Track metrics such as the number of records processed, the number of records processed after the last high-water mark, and the number of records that were skipped because they were already processed before the last high-water mark.
- Use a library or framework that supports high-water mark tracking.

Real-world examples:

- Apache Kafka uses the High-Water Mark pattern to track the progress of data consumption by consumers.
- Apache Storm uses the High-Water Mark pattern to track the progress of data processing by bolts.

Hybrid Clock

Hybrid Clock is a system design pattern that combines both a logical clock and a physical clock to provide a more accurate way of ordering events in a distributed system. Logical clocks are used to order events within a single node, while physical clocks are used to order events across multiple nodes.

The Hybrid Clock pattern uses a combination of both logical and physical clocks to provide a more accurate way of ordering events, as well as to handle clock drift and network delays. The logical clock is based on the number of events that have occurred within a node, while the physical clock is based on the current time as reported by the system's clock.

The Hybrid Clock pattern is often used in distributed systems that require strong consistency, such as distributed databases and distributed file systems. Companies such as Google and Yahoo have used this pattern in their distributed systems to provide accurate ordering of events.

Trade-offs:

- It can add complexity to the system as it requires maintaining both logical and physical clocks.

- It may require additional computation to maintain and synchronize the clocks.

Best Practices:

- Monitor the clock drift and network delays to ensure that the Hybrid Clock is providing accurate ordering of events.
- Use a library or framework that provides an implementation of the Hybrid Clock pattern.

Real-world examples:

- Google's Spanner distributed database uses a Hybrid Clock for accurate ordering of events.
- Yahoo's PNUTS distributed database uses a Hybrid Clock for accurate ordering of events.
- Apache Cassandra uses a Hybrid Clock for accurate ordering of events in its distributed database.

Idempotent Receiver

The Idempotent Receiver pattern is a system design pattern that is used to ensure that a message is only processed once, even if it is delivered multiple times. This pattern is often used in systems that rely on message-based communication, such as microservices and event-driven architectures.

The Idempotent Receiver pattern is implemented by assigning a unique identifier to each message, such as a message ID or a timestamp. When a message is received, the receiver checks if the message has been processed before by looking up the unique identifier in a message store. If the message has already been processed, it is ignored. If the message has not been processed, it is processed and the unique identifier is added to the message store.

This pattern is useful in systems where messages may be lost or delayed, and can help prevent duplicate processing of messages. It can also be used in situations where a message may be sent multiple times due to a network or system failure.

Companies such as Netflix and Uber have implemented the Idempotent Receiver pattern in their microservice architectures to ensure that messages are only processed once.

Trade-offs:

- it will add extra latency to the system as it will have to check the message store before processing the message.
- it will add extra memory usage to the system as it will have to keep track of the message store.

Best Practices:

- Use a unique identifier that is guaranteed to be unique and cannot be easily replicated.
- Choose a message store that is fast and scalable, such as a distributed cache.
- Implement a cleanup mechanism to remove old entries from the message store.

Real-world examples:

- Netflix's Eureka service registry uses the Idempotent Receiver pattern to ensure that instances are only registered once.
- Kafka, a popular message queue, provides support for the Idempotent Receiver pattern through its built-in duplicate detection feature.

- Apache Camel, an open-source integration framework, provides support for the Idempotent Receiver pattern through its Idempotent Consumer feature.

Index Table

The Index Table pattern is a way of organizing data in a database to optimize the performance of queries. It involves creating a separate table that contains a subset of the data in the original table, organized in a way that makes it easier to find specific rows. This table is called an index table, and it is used to speed up the process of finding and retrieving data from the original table.

The index table is typically created based on the most commonly used fields in queries, such as the primary key or a specific column that is frequently searched for. The index table will contain a copy of the indexed field, as well as a pointer to the corresponding row in the original table. When a query is made, the index table is searched first, and the pointer is used to retrieve the relevant data from the original table.

This pattern is commonly used in relational databases, such as MySQL, PostgreSQL, and Oracle, to improve the performance of SELECT queries. Companies such as Amazon and Google use the Index Table pattern to improve the performance of their databases and ensure fast and efficient data retrieval for their users.

Trade-offs:

- It will increase the storage and memory usage as it will have to keep a copy of indexed fields in the index table
- It will increase the complexity of the system as it requires additional maintenance and updates to the index table

Best Practices:

- Regularly analyze the queries and select the most frequently used fields as the indexed fields.
- Periodically update the index table to keep it in sync with the original table.
- Use a database management system that supports indexing and has built-in tools for managing index tables.

Real-world examples:

- MySQL, PostgreSQL, and Oracle databases all support index tables.
- Amazon DynamoDB uses index tables to improve the performance of its NoSQL database service.
- Google's Bigtable uses index tables to improve the performance of its distributed NoSQL database service.

Key-Range Partitions

The Key-Range Partitions pattern is used to partition data in a distributed system based on the key values of the data. Each partition is responsible for a range of key values, allowing for efficient data retrieval and management. This pattern is commonly used in distributed databases and key-value stores.

For example, in a distributed database that stores customer information, the keys could be customer IDs. The keys are then partitioned into ranges, such as 1-1000, 1001-2000, etc. Each partition is responsible for managing the data for the keys within its assigned range. This allows for efficient data retrieval and management, as well as easy scalability by adding or removing partitions as necessary.

Companies such as Amazon's DynamoDB and Google's Bigtable use the Key-Range Partitions pattern in their distributed databases.

Trade-offs:

- It can be difficult to determine the appropriate key ranges and partition sizes for a given system, as it depends on the specific data and usage patterns.

- Rebalancing partitions can be a complex and resource-intensive process.

Best Practices:

- Monitor key distribution and adjust partition ranges as needed to maintain an even distribution of keys across partitions.
- Use consistent hashing to distribute keys across partitions to minimize the impact of adding or removing partitions.
- Use a partitioning library that supports dynamic partitioning and rebalancing.

Real-world examples:

- Amazon's DynamoDB uses the Key-Range Partitions pattern to partition data in its distributed database.
- Google's Bigtable also uses Key-Range Partitions pattern to partition data in its distributed database.

Leader Election

Leader Election is a system design pattern used in distributed systems to elect a leader among a group of peers. The leader is responsible for coordinating the actions of the group and making decisions on behalf of the group. The leader is typically elected through a consensus algorithm, such as Paxos or Raft.

The leader is responsible for maintaining the state of the system and handling incoming requests. It also ensures that the state of the system is consistent among all the peers. In case of leader failure, a new leader is elected. This ensures that the system can still function even if one of the peers fails.

Trade-offs:

- It increases the complexity of the system as it needs to handle the leader election and failure detection.
- It introduces a single point of failure.

Best Practices:

- Monitor the state of the leader election process to ensure that it is functioning as expected.
- Implement a leader election algorithm that can handle network partitions.

- Monitor the performance of the system when a leader change occurs.

Real-world examples:

- Apache ZooKeeper, a distributed coordination service, uses leader election to elect a leader among the ensemble of servers.
- Kafka, a distributed streaming platform, uses leader election to elect a leader for each partition of a topic.
- Etcd, a distributed key-value store, uses leader election to elect a leader among the members of the cluster.

Leader and Followers

Leader and Followers is a design pattern used in distributed systems to handle coordination and communication between multiple nodes or processes. The pattern involves selecting a leader node, which is responsible for coordinating the actions of the other nodes, known as followers.

In this pattern, the leader node is responsible for coordinating tasks, such as data replication and communication between nodes. The followers listen to the leader and execute tasks based on the leader's instructions. In case the leader node fails, the followers will elect a new leader to take its place. This ensures that there is always a node in charge of coordinating the actions of the other nodes, even in the event of a failure.

This pattern is commonly used in distributed databases, where the leader node coordinates the replication of data to the followers. Companies such as Apache Cassandra and Apache Zookeeper use the Leader and Followers pattern to handle coordination and data replication in their distributed systems.

Trade-offs:

- Having a single leader node can create a bottleneck in the system as all requests must pass through the leader node.

- If the leader node fails, there may be a delay in electing a new leader, which can cause a temporary disruption in the system.

Best Practices:

- Implement a mechanism for quickly electing a new leader in case the current leader fails.
- Monitor the state of the leader node and be prepared to quickly detect and respond to a failure.
- Consider using a leader election library to handle the complexity of the leader election process.

Real-world examples:

- Apache Cassandra uses the Leader and Followers pattern to handle data replication and coordination in its distributed database system.
- Apache Zookeeper uses the Leader and Followers pattern to handle coordination and communication between nodes in its distributed system.

- Raft, a consensus algorithm, uses the Leader and Followers pattern to handle coordination and data replication in distributed systems.

Lease

A lease is a system design pattern that is used to manage access to shared resources in a distributed system. It is a way of ensuring that only one node or entity has access to a resource at a time, and that access is granted for a specific period of time.

A lease is granted to a node or entity by a lease grantor, typically a central lease manager. The node or entity can then use the resource for the duration of the lease, after which it must be renewed or returned. If the lease is not renewed, the resource is made available for other nodes or entities to acquire.

Leases can be used for a variety of resources, such as shared storage, network bandwidth, and processing power. For example, a distributed file system might use leases to ensure that only one node can write to a file at a time, while a distributed database might use leases to ensure that only one node can access a specific piece of data at a time.

Leases can be implemented using a variety of algorithms, such as Lease-Based Locking or Paxos. Companies such as Google and Microsoft have used leases to manage access to shared resources in their distributed systems.

Trade-offs:

- Leases can add extra overhead to the system as they require a central lease manager and a mechanism for renewing leases.

- Leases can introduce contention for resources if multiple nodes or entities try to acquire the same lease at the same time.

Best Practices:

- Implement a lease timeout mechanism to ensure that leases are not held indefinitely.

- Implement a mechanism for renewing leases to avoid contention for resources.

- Monitor the state of leases to ensure that they are being acquired and released as expected.

Real-world examples:

- Google's Chubby distributed lock service uses leases to manage access to shared resources in the Google File System.

- Apache Zookeeper, a distributed coordination service, uses leases to manage access to shared resources.

- Microsoft's Azure Cosmos DB uses leases to manage access to shared resources in the distributed database.

Low-Water Mark

The Low-Water Mark pattern is a system design pattern used in distributed systems to ensure that resources are not over-allocated. The pattern is often used in resource management systems, such as memory or disk space management, to track the amount of available resources and prevent over-allocation.

The Low-Water Mark is a threshold value that represents the minimum amount of resources that must be available at all times. When the system detects that the amount of available resources has fallen below the Low-Water Mark, it will trigger an event or alert to notify the system administrator or resource manager. This allows the administrator to take action, such as releasing resources or allocating more, to ensure that the system remains operational.

The Low-Water Mark pattern is often used in conjunction with the High-Water Mark pattern, which sets a threshold for the maximum amount of resources that can be allocated. Together, the High-Water Mark and Low-Water Mark provide a way to ensure that resources are used efficiently, without over-allocating or under-allocating.

Trade-offs:

- There is an overhead in maintaining and monitoring the low-water mark threshold.
- If the low-water mark is set too low, it may trigger false alarms or cause the system to release resources too early.

Best Practices:

- Set the low-water mark threshold based on the specific requirements and constraints of the system.
- Monitor resource usage and adjust the low-water mark threshold as needed.
- Use monitoring and alerting tools to detect when the low-water mark is breached.
- Test the low-water mark threshold in a staging environment before deploying to production.

Real-world examples:

- Apache Cassandra uses low-water mark to handle memory management and prevent over-allocation of resources.
- Redis uses low-water mark to handle memory management and prevent the over-allocation of resources.
- Kubernetes uses low-water mark to handle CPU and memory allocation in containers.

Materialized View

The Materialized View pattern is a way to store the results of a query as a separate, pre-computed table. This table can be updated periodically to reflect the current state of the data, and can be queried directly, rather than having to run the query each time it is needed.

This pattern is commonly used in data warehousing and business intelligence systems, where the data is large and complex and performance is a concern. By pre-computing the results of a query, the system can respond to queries more quickly, and can also handle a higher query load.

For example, a retail company might use a Materialized View to store the results of a query that aggregates sales data by product category, so that analysts can quickly access this information without having to run the query each time.

Trade-offs:

- Additional storage and computation resources are required to maintain the Materialized View
- Refreshing the view can add latency to the system

- Additional complexity is added to the system to maintain the Materialized View

Best practices:

- Use Materialized View when dealing with large amounts of data that needs to be queried frequently.
- Refresh the Materialized View on regular intervals to keep the data up to date.
- Make sure to have proper indexing on the Materialized View.

Real-world examples:

- Amazon Redshift, a data warehouse service, uses Materialized Views to improve query performance.
- Oracle Database, a relational database management system, also supports Materialized Views.

Paxos

Paxos is a distributed consensus algorithm that allows a group of processes to agree on a value in a fault-tolerant manner. The algorithm is named after the Paxos island in Greece where the problem of reaching consensus was first described by Leslie Lamport in a series of papers in the late 1990s.

The basic idea behind Paxos is that a group of processes can agree on a value by reaching consensus on a series of rounds of communication. In each round, a process called the leader proposes a value, and the other processes, called acceptors, vote on whether to accept the proposed value. If a majority of acceptors vote to accept the value, the consensus is reached, and the value is chosen as the final agreed-upon value.

Paxos is used in a variety of distributed systems, including databases, file systems, and messaging systems. For example, the distributed database system Google Spanner uses Paxos to ensure consistency in its globally distributed data. Some popular implementation of Paxos include Apache ZooKeeper, Google's Chubby, and etcd.

The Paxos algorithm is known for its reliability and fault-tolerance, but it can be challenging to implement in practice.

One of the main challenges is ensuring that the leader and acceptors communicate reliably, which can be difficult in a distributed system where network partitions and failures are common. Additionally, Paxos requires a significant amount of coordination between the processes, which can lead to high overhead and complexity in the implementation.

Trade-offs:

- It is relatively complex to implement and reason about.
- It can be challenging to guarantee that the leader and acceptors communicate reliably in a distributed system.
- It requires a significant amount of coordination between the processes, which can lead to high overhead and complexity in the implementation.

Best Practices:

- Use a pre-existing Paxos implementation, such as Apache ZooKeeper, Google's Chubby, etcd.
- Monitor and tune the performance of your Paxos implementation to ensure that it meets your requirements.
- Consider using a simpler consensus algorithm, such as Raft, in situations where Paxos is too complex or overkill.

Real-world examples:

- Google Spanner uses Paxos to ensure consistency in its globally distributed data.
- Apache ZooKeeper and etcd use Paxos as a core component of their distributed coordination

Priority Queue

The Priority Queue pattern is a system design pattern that is used to prioritize and manage the processing of tasks or requests within a system. This pattern is often used in systems that have a high volume of requests or tasks that need to be processed in a specific order.

The Priority Queue pattern works by assigning a priority level to each task or request. The tasks or requests are then placed into a queue, with the tasks or requests with the highest priority level at the front of the queue, and the tasks or requests with the lowest priority level at the back of the queue. When the system is ready to process a task or request, it will always take the task or request at the front of the queue, ensuring that the highest priority tasks or requests are processed first.

The Priority Queue pattern can be implemented using a variety of data structures such as a heap or a queue with multiple levels of priority. Some systems also use a combination of data structures, such as a combination of a heap and a queue, to implement the pattern.

Companies such as Amazon and Google use the Priority Queue pattern in their systems to ensure that high-priority tasks or requests are processed as quickly as possible. For example, Amazon's order processing system uses the Priority Queue pattern to ensure that high-priority orders are processed and shipped first.

Trade-offs:

- It can be difficult to set the right priority levels for tasks or requests, which may lead to some tasks or requests being overlooked or delayed.
- It can be complex to implement the pattern, especially when using multiple data structures to implement it.

Best Practices:

- Set clear priority levels for tasks or requests and communicate them clearly to the team.
- Monitor the queue to ensure that tasks or requests are being processed in the correct order.
- Regularly review the priority levels and adjust them as needed.
- Use a Priority Queue library or framework to simplify the implementation of the pattern.

Real-world examples:

- Amazon's order processing system uses the Priority Queue pattern to ensure that high-priority orders are processed and shipped first.

- Google's search engine uses the Priority Queue pattern to prioritize and process search queries in real-time.

- Apache Kafka uses the Priority Queue pattern to prioritize and process messages in real-time.

Proactor System

Proactor system pattern is a design pattern used for handling I/O-bound and high-concurrency scenarios. It is based on the Proactor design pattern, which separates the concerns of event handling and event demultiplexing. In a Proactor system, an event demultiplexer (or Proactor) is responsible for monitoring multiple I/O handles and notifying the appropriate event handler when an event occurs.

The Proactor pattern uses an asynchronous approach, where the event handler is notified when an event occurs, and then it can perform the required action without blocking the Proactor. This allows for better scalability and efficient use of resources, as the Proactor can handle multiple events simultaneously without blocking.

One example of a Proactor system is the Windows Operating System's I/O Completion Ports (IOCP) API. It allows multiple threads to handle I/O operations simultaneously, without blocking the main thread. This allows for better scalability and efficient use of resources.

Another example is the libuv library, which is a multi-platform support library with a focus on asynchronous I/O. It provides an event loop, thread pool, and other abstractions to support Proactor pattern.

Trade-offs:

- Proactor systems can be more complex to implement and understand, as the asynchronous nature of the pattern can make the code more difficult to follow.
- They may also require more resources, such as memory and CPU, to handle multiple events simultaneously.

Best Practices:

- Use an existing Proactor implementation, such as the IOCP API or libuv, to reduce the complexity of implementation.
- Monitor the performance of the Proactor system to ensure that it is handling events efficiently and effectively.
- Use Proactor pattern with other design patterns such as Circuit Breaker and CQRS to improve the fault tolerance and scalability of the system.

Real-world examples:

- Windows Operating System's I/O Completion Ports (IOCP) API

- libuv library

- Boost.Asio C++ library

- The Proactor pattern is used in many high-performance servers and networking libraries.

Publisher/Subscriber

The Publisher/Subscriber pattern is a messaging pattern where a central message broker (the publisher) sends messages to multiple subscribers. The subscribers register with the broker and receive messages that are relevant to them. This pattern is often used in distributed systems to decouple components and allow for more flexible and scalable communication.

In this pattern, the publisher sends messages to a message broker, which then distributes the messages to the subscribers. The subscribers can either pull messages from the broker or have the messages pushed to them. This pattern allows for multiple components to receive the same message, without any of them needing to know about the other components.

Real-world examples:

- Apache Kafka is a popular open-source message broker that uses the publisher/subscriber pattern.
- RabbitMQ is another popular open-source message broker that supports the publisher/subscriber pattern.
- Many cloud providers, such as AWS and Azure, have their own message broker services that use the publisher/subscriber pattern.

Trade-offs:

- The publisher/subscriber pattern can add complexity to a system, as it requires a separate message broker and additional logic for registering and managing subscribers.
- In some cases, it can add latency to the system, as messages may need to be sent to a broker and then distributed to subscribers.

Best practices:

- Use a message broker that is designed for high performance and scalability.
- Use message acknowledgements to ensure that messages have been successfully received by subscribers.
- Use message persistence to ensure that messages are not lost in the case of a broker or subscriber failure.
- Monitor the message broker and subscribers to ensure that messages are being processed in a timely manne

Queue-Based Load Leveling

The Queue-Based Load Leveling pattern is used to balance workloads and prevent overloading of a system by using a queue to buffer incoming requests. This pattern is often used in systems that need to handle a large number of requests, such as web applications.

When a request arrives, it is added to a queue. The system then processes requests from the queue, one at a time. This allows the system to handle bursts of requests without overloading the system, as requests can be temporarily stored in the queue and processed at a later time.

This pattern can be used in combination with other patterns, such as load balancing or rate limiting, to further improve the performance and scalability of a system.

Trade-offs:

- adding a queue may add latency to the system, as requests have to wait in the queue before being processed.
- it may also require additional resources, such as memory, to store the requests in the queue.

Best Practices:

- Use a message queue that supports auto-scaling, so that the queue can grow or shrink based on the number of requests.

- Monitor the queue to ensure that it is not becoming a bottleneck or causing delays.

- Use a message queue that supports prioritization or fairness so that requests are processed in the order they were received.

- It is important to design the queue size, and the rate at which it is consumed, based on the expected traffic and the processing power of the system.

Real-world examples:

- Amazon's Simple Queue Service (SQS) is a managed message queue service that implements the Queue-Based Load Leveling pattern.

- RabbitMQ is a popular open-source message queue that can be used to implement the Queue-Based Load Leveling pattern.

Quorum

Quorum is a system design pattern that is used in distributed systems to ensure that a majority of the nodes in the system are in agreement before making a decision or performing an action. The quorum is typically defined as a majority of the nodes in the system, but the specific number of nodes required can vary depending on the system's requirements and configuration.

The quorum pattern is used to ensure that a decision or action is taken by a sufficient number of nodes to ensure that it is correct and that the system remains consistent. This is especially important in systems that use replication and failover, where multiple copies of the data are maintained across different nodes.

Quorum-based systems are typically used in distributed databases, distributed file systems, and other types of distributed systems where data consistency and availability are critical. Companies such as Google, Amazon, and Microsoft use quorum-based systems to ensure the availability and consistency of their data in distributed systems.

Trade-offs:

- It can lead to a decrease in performance of the system as it will have to wait for the quorum to be reached before making a decision or performing an action.
- It can lead to an increase in complexity of the system as it will have to keep track of the state of the nodes in the system.

Best Practices:

- Choose a quorum size that is large enough to ensure that the system remains available and consistent, but small enough to minimize the impact on performance.
- Monitor the state of the quorum to ensure that it is being reached as expected.
- Ensure that the quorum algorithm is fault-tolerant and can handle the failure of nodes.

Real-world examples:

- Google's Spanner database uses a quorum-based system to ensure the consistency and availability of its data.
- Amazon's DynamoDB uses a quorum-based system to ensure the consistency and availability of its data.
- Apache Cassandra uses a quorum-based system to ensure the consistency and availability of its data.

Rate Limiting

Rate limiting is a pattern used to control the rate at which a system can be accessed or a specific action can be performed. It is used to prevent abuse or overuse of a system by limiting the number of requests that a user or system can make within a specified time frame.

Rate limiting can be implemented in a variety of ways, such as token bucket or leaky bucket algorithms, which both use a token-based approach to limit the rate at which requests can be made. Tokens are added to the bucket at a specific rate, and each request consumes a token. If there are no tokens available, the request is denied.

Another approach is the fixed window algorithm, which keeps track of the number of requests made within a fixed time window and denies requests if the limit is exceeded.

Rate limiting can be applied at different levels in a system, such as at the network level, application level, or at the user level. It can be useful for protecting against DDoS attacks, preventing abuse of an API, or controlling resource usage in a distributed system.

Trade-offs:

- It can limit the throughput of the system
- can cause inconvenience for legitimate users if the limit is set too low

Best Practices:

- Implement rate limiting at the network level for maximum effectiveness.
- Use different rate limits for different types of requests.
- Monitor rate limiting metrics to ensure that the system is performing as expected.
- Provide clear error messages and guidance for users when rate limits are exceeded.
- Use a distributed rate limiting system to handle a high number of requests.

Real-world examples:

- Cloudflare's rate limiting service is used to protect against DDoS attacks and abuse of APIs.
- AWS provides rate limiting capabilities through its API Gateway service.
- GitHub uses rate limiting to prevent abuse of its API and protect its servers.

Reactive System

he Reactive System pattern is a design approach that focuses on building systems that are highly responsive, resilient, and elastic. This pattern is based on the Reactive Manifesto, which defines four key characteristics that a reactive system should have: responsiveness, elasticity, resilience, and message-driven.

Responsiveness: A reactive system should respond to changes in the environment in a timely manner, providing a fast and consistent user experience.

Elasticity: A reactive system should be able to scale up or down as needed, handling a varying number of requests without compromising performance.

Resilience: A reactive system should be able to handle failures and recover quickly, without disrupting the overall system.

Message-driven: A reactive system should rely on asynchronous message passing to communicate between components, allowing for loose coupling and increased scalability.

Reactive systems are commonly used in systems that require high scalability and low latency, such as real-time streaming data, online gaming, and social media platforms. Companies such as Twitter,

Netflix, and LinkedIn have implemented the Reactive System pattern to improve the performance and scalability of their systems.

Trade-offs:

- A reactive system requires a different mindset and programming model compared to traditional systems, which can be challenging to implement and maintain.
- Reactive systems may require more resources to handle the increased communication between components.

Best Practices:

- Use a Reactive programming framework such as Spring Reactor or Akka.
- Use non-blocking I/O to handle high concurrency.
- Use an event-driven architecture to communicate between components.
- Use circuit breakers to handle failures.

Real-world examples:

- Twitter has implemented a reactive system using the Scala programming language and the Akka framework to handle the high volume of tweets and user interactions.

- Netflix uses the Reactive System pattern to handle the streaming of movies and TV shows to millions of customers.
- LinkedIn uses a reactive system to handle the high volume of data generated by its users, such as messages, updates, and job postings.

Reactor System

The Reactive System pattern is a design pattern that allows for the building of systems that are highly responsive, resilient, and elastic. This pattern is based on the Reactive Manifesto, which defines a set of principles for building systems that are responsive to the needs of users and the environment.

One of the key principles of the Reactive System pattern is that systems should be able to react to changes in their environment in a timely and efficient manner. This means that systems should be able to handle large numbers of concurrent requests, recover quickly from failures, and scale up or down based on demand.

Another principle of the Reactive System pattern is that systems should be message-driven, meaning that they should use asynchronous messaging to communicate between components. This allows for loose coupling between components and can help improve the resilience of the system.

The Reactive System pattern can be applied to a wide range of systems, including web applications, mobile apps, and IoT systems. Companies such as Netflix, Twitter, and PayPal have implemented the Reactive System pattern to improve the performance and scalability of their systems.

Trade-offs:

- The Reactive System pattern can be more complex to implement than traditional synchronous systems.
- It can require a significant change in the way developers think about and build systems.

Best Practices:

- Design your system to be message-driven and use asynchronous messaging to communicate between components.
- Use a library or framework that supports the Reactive System pattern, such as Akka, Reactor, or RxJava.
- Monitor the system to ensure that it is performing as expected and make adjustments as necessary.
- Consider the use of a service mesh to manage service discovery, load balancing, and other aspects of service communication.

Real-world examples:

- Netflix uses the Reactive System pattern in their streaming service to handle large numbers of concurrent requests and to improve the performance and scalability of the system.

- Twitter uses the Reactive System pattern in their backend systems to handle high levels of traffic and to improve the responsiveness of the service.

- Paypal uses the Reactive System pattern in their mobile app to improve the responsiveness and performance of the app.

Recircular Queue-based Load Leveling

The Recircular Queue-based Load Leveling pattern is a way to handle incoming requests in a distributed system. The pattern uses a circular queue to store incoming requests, with the goal of distributing the requests evenly among a group of worker threads.

When a request comes in, it is added to the circular queue. A worker thread will then take the request from the front of the queue and process it. Once the request is processed, the worker thread will add it to the back of the queue. This allows for the requests to be distributed evenly among the worker threads, ensuring that no single thread becomes overwhelmed with requests.

The Recircular Queue-based Load Leveling pattern can be useful in systems that receive a high volume of requests, such as web servers or message queues. Companies such as Twitter and Netflix have implemented this pattern to handle incoming requests and distribute them evenly among a group of worker threads.

Trade-offs:

- It can add extra latency to the system as requests need to be added to the queue before being processed.

- It can add extra memory usage to the system as the queue needs to be stored in memory.

Best Practices:

- Monitor the length of the queue to ensure that it does not become too long.
- Adjust the number of worker threads based on the specific needs of the system.
- Use a thread-safe implementation of the circular queue.

Real-world examples:

- Twitter's Finagle library includes an implementation of the Recircular Queue-based Load Leveling pattern.
- Apache Cassandra, a distributed NoSQL database, uses a Recircular Queue-based Load Leveling pattern to handle incoming requests and distribute them evenly among a group of worker threads.

Replicated Log

The Replicated Log pattern is a way to ensure consistency and fault tolerance in distributed systems. The pattern uses a log that is replicated across multiple nodes in the system, with each node having a copy of the log. When a node makes a change to the log, it is responsible for replicating that change to all other nodes in the system.

This pattern is commonly used in distributed databases and messaging systems. For example, Apache Kafka and Apache Cassandra use the Replicated Log pattern to ensure data consistency and fault tolerance. The pattern is also used in distributed systems that require strong consistency, such as financial systems.

Trade-offs:

- It can add extra latency to the system as the changes need to be replicated to all nodes.
- It can add extra load to the system as the nodes need to constantly check for updates and replicate changes.

Best Practices:

- Use a library or framework that supports the Replicated Log pattern, such as Apache Kafka or Apache Cassandra.

- Monitor the state of the Replicated Log to ensure that all nodes have the latest updates.

- Configure the replication factor to meet the specific needs of the system.

Real-world examples:

- Apache Kafka uses the Replicated Log pattern to ensure fault-tolerance and high-throughput in its messaging system.

- Apache Cassandra uses the Replicated Log pattern to ensure consistency and fault-tolerance in its distributed database.

- Raft is a consensus algorithm that uses the Replicated Log pattern to ensure consistency and fault-tolerance in distributed systems.

Request Batch

The Request Batch pattern is a way to optimize the performance of a system by grouping multiple requests into a single batch and processing them together. This can be done in a number of ways, such as by combining multiple small requests into a single larger request, or by processing multiple requests in parallel.

One common use case for the Request Batch pattern is in distributed systems where multiple clients are making requests to a shared resource, such as a database. By batching requests, the system can reduce the number of round trips between the clients and the resource, which can result in significant performance improvements.

Another use case is in systems that process large amounts of data, such as data pipelines or data lakes. By batching requests, the system can improve the throughput and reduce the latency of data processing.

Companies such as Google and Amazon have implemented the Request Batch pattern in various parts of their systems, such as in their data processing pipelines and in their cloud storage services.

Trade-offs:

- Batching requests can increase the complexity of the system, as it can be difficult to maintain consistency and ordering of requests.
- Batching requests can also increase the risk of failure, as a single failed request can cause an entire batch to fail.

Best Practices:

- Monitor the system to ensure that the batch size is optimal, and adjust as needed.
- Provide a mechanism to handle failed requests in the batch.
- Ensure that the system can handle large batches of requests, and that it can scale as needed.

Real-world examples:

- Amazon S3 uses the Request Batch pattern to improve the performance of its data storage service.
- Google Cloud Dataflow uses the Request Batch pattern to improve the performance of its data processing pipeline.
- Apache Hadoop's MapReduce framework uses the Request Batch pattern to process large amounts of data in parallel.

Request Pipeline

The Request Pipeline pattern is a way to organize the processing of requests in a system. It involves breaking down the processing of a request into a series of smaller, reusable steps or stages. Each stage is responsible for a specific aspect of the processing, such as validation, authentication, authorization, and business logic.

The Request Pipeline pattern is commonly used in web applications, where the processing of a request involves multiple layers of logic, such as routing, middleware, controllers, and services. The pipeline pattern is used to organize the flow of request and response, by breaking it down into smaller, reusable pieces, and allowing different stages to be composed together in a flexible way.

The Request Pipeline pattern can be implemented in different ways, depending on the technology stack and architecture of the system. In a web application, it can be implemented using middleware, which is a layer of code that sits between the web server and the application logic. Middleware can be used to add functionality to a request, such as logging, authentication, and validation, before it reaches the application logic.

Trade-offs:

- It can add complexity to the system as it requires breaking down the logic into smaller, reusable pieces.
- It can increase the number of dependencies between the different stages of the pipeline.

Best Practices:

- Keep the pipeline stages small and focused on a specific aspect of the processing.
- Use a consistent naming and ordering convention for the pipeline stages.
- Use a pipeline library that supports configurable ordering and composition of pipeline stages.
- Provide clear documentation and instructions for extending and customizing the pipeline

Real-world examples:

- ASP.NET Core uses a middleware pipeline to handle requests and responses.
- Express.js, a popular web framework for Node.js, uses a middleware pipeline to handle requests and responses.

Request Waiting List

Request Waiting List is a system design pattern that is used to handle a high number of requests to a system or service. It works by creating a list of requests that are waiting to be processed and then handling them in a first-in-first-out (FIFO) order. This pattern helps to ensure that all requests are handled in a fair and consistent manner, regardless of their order of arrival.

One example of the Request Waiting List pattern is a web server that receives a large number of requests from users. The server creates a waiting list of requests and processes them one at a time, ensuring that no single request is handled before all others. This pattern is also commonly used in messaging systems, where messages are added to a queue and processed in the order they were received.

Trade-offs:

- It may increase the latency of the system if the number of requests is high and the processing time of each request is long.
- It may increase the memory usage of the system if a large number of requests need to be stored in the waiting list.

Best Practices:

- Implement a priority system to handle urgent requests first.

- Implement a mechanism to handle expired requests.

- Monitor the waiting list to ensure that requests are being handled in a timely manner.

- Implement a mechanism to handle failed requests.

Real-world examples:

- Amazon SQS is a messaging service that uses the Request Waiting List pattern to handle messages.

- RabbitMQ is a messaging broker that uses the Request Waiting List pattern to handle messages.

- Apache Kafka is a distributed streaming platform that uses the Request Waiting List pattern to handle messages.

Resource Pool

The Resource Pool pattern is a system design pattern that manages a pool of resources, such as connections to a database or network connections. The pattern is used to limit the number of resources that are created and to reuse resources that are no longer in use. This can help to improve the performance and scalability of a system by reducing the overhead of creating and destroying resources, and by making more efficient use of resources that are already created.

The Resource Pool pattern typically includes a pool of resources, a mechanism for acquiring and releasing resources, and a mechanism for monitoring and managing the pool of resources. When a resource is needed, it is acquired from the pool. When it is no longer needed, it is released back to the pool. If all resources in the pool are in use, the system may either block until a resource becomes available or create a new resource, depending on the implementation. If a resource is not used for a certain amount of time, it may be closed or removed from the pool.

The Resource Pool pattern can be used in a variety of systems, such as database connection pools, thread pools, and network connection pools. Companies such as Oracle and Microsoft have implemented resource pooling in their database management systems.

Trade-offs:

- Managing a pool of resources can add complexity to a system, and may require additional memory and processing resources.
- If the pool is not configured correctly or is not properly managed, it can lead to resource contention or resource leakage.

Best Practices:

- Monitor the pool to ensure that it is sized correctly and that resources are being reused efficiently.
- Set up alerts to notify the administrator when the pool is running low on resources.
- Use a Resource Pool library that provides monitoring and management capabilities.

Real-world examples:

- Oracle's Universal Connection Pool (UCP) is a resource pool that manages database connections.

- The Apache Commons DBCP library provides a connection pool for database connections.
- The Java ThreadPoolExecutor class provides a thread pool that can be used to manage threads in a system.

Retry

The Retry pattern is used to handle transient failures in remote service calls by retrying the failed request a specified number of times before giving up and returning an error to the caller. This pattern can help improve the resiliency of a distributed system by handling temporary failures, such as network outages or server overloads.

When a service call fails, the Retry pattern waits for a specified period of time before retrying the request. If the request fails again, the Retry pattern waits for a longer period of time before retrying again. This process continues until the request is successful or the maximum number of retries is reached. If the maximum number of retries is reached, the Retry pattern returns an error to the caller.

The Retry pattern can be useful for systems that make a large number of remote service calls, such as microservice architectures. Companies such as Amazon and Google have implemented the Retry pattern to improve the resiliency of their distributed systems.

Trade-offs:

- It will add extra latency to the system as it will have to wait before retrying a request.
- It will add extra load to the system as it will have to retry the same request multiple times.

Best Practices:

- Use a back-off algorithm to gradually increase the time between retries.
- Keep track of the number of retries, the time between retries, and the results of each retry.
- Use a Retry library that supports configurable retry counts and back-off algorithms.

Real-world examples:

- Amazon's AWS SDK includes support for the Retry pattern through the AWS SDK Retry Client.
- GCP's Cloud SDK includes support for the Retry pattern through the Cloud SDK Retry Wrapper.
- The Apache HTTP Client library includes support for the Retry pattern through the HttpRequestRetryHandler interface.

Saga

The Saga pattern is a way to manage long-running, distributed transactions in a microservices architecture. It is based on the idea that a transaction can be broken down into a series of smaller transactions, each of which can be executed independently. The Saga pattern allows for the coordination of these smaller transactions, ensuring that they are executed in the correct order and that any errors are handled correctly.

The Saga pattern is implemented using a Saga Manager, which is responsible for managing the state of the distributed transactions. The Saga Manager sends commands to the individual services involved in the transaction, and each service responds with the status of the command. The Saga Manager uses this information to determine the overall state of the transaction and to decide what the next step should be.

In case of failure, the Saga Manager uses the compensating transactions to undo the previous steps and bring the system back to a consistent state.

The Saga pattern is useful for systems that need to maintain data consistency across multiple services, such as e-commerce systems or financial systems. Companies such as Uber and PayPal have used the Saga pattern to improve the reliability of their distributed systems.

Trade-offs:

- It can add complexity to the system as it requires coordination between multiple services.
- It can add additional latency as it requires multiple roundtrips between the Saga manager and the services.
- It can increase the risk of data inconsistency if the compensating transactions are not implemented correctly.

Best Practices:

- Keep the Sagas small and focused on a specific business transaction
- Use idempotent compensating transactions
- Monitor the state of the Sagas to ensure that they are executing as expected.
- Test the Sagas in isolation and in conjunction with the other services.

Real-world examples:

- PayPal uses Saga pattern to manage the distributed transactions across multiple services.

- Uber uses Saga pattern to handle the distributed transactions in their payment service.
- Axon Framework provides support for implementing the Saga pattern in the microservice architecture.

Scale-Out

The Scale-Out pattern is a method of increasing the capacity and performance of a system by adding more nodes (or instances) to the system. This pattern is often used in distributed systems and cloud-based systems to handle increased traffic and load.

The Scale-Out pattern can be implemented in a number of ways, such as by using load balancers to distribute traffic across multiple nodes, or by using auto-scaling to dynamically add and remove nodes based on the current load.

Companies such as Amazon and Google use the Scale-Out pattern in their cloud services, such as Amazon Web Services (AWS) and Google Cloud Platform (GCP), to handle the large number of requests and the variability of workloads.

Trade-offs:

- Scale-Out can be more expensive than Scale-Up, as it requires more resources (such as servers or instances) to handle the increased load.
- Scale-Out can also be more complex to manage and monitor, as it requires coordination and communication between the multiple nodes in the system.

Best Practices:

- Use load balancers to distribute traffic evenly across the nodes in the system.

- Use auto-scaling to dynamically add and remove nodes based on the current load.

- Monitor the system's performance and capacity to ensure that it can handle the expected traffic and load.

- Use monitoring and alerting tools to detect and respond to performance bottlenecks or capacity issues.

- Use a configuration management tool to automate the deployment and configuration of new nodes in the system.

Real-world examples:

- Amazon Web Services (AWS) uses the Scale-Out pattern in its cloud services, such as Amazon Elastic Compute Cloud (EC2) and Amazon Elastic Container Service (ECS), to handle the large number of requests and the variability of workloads.

- Google Cloud Platform (GCP) uses the Scale-Out pattern in its cloud services, such as Google Compute Engine (GCE) and Google Kubernetes Engine (GKE), to handle the large number of requests and the variability of workloads.

- Netflix uses the Scale-Out pattern in its microservice-based architecture to handle the large number of requests and the variability of workloads.

Scheduled-task

The Scheduled-task pattern is a design pattern for scheduling and executing tasks on a regular basis. This pattern is commonly used in systems that need to perform certain actions at specific intervals, such as data backups, data cleaning, and data processing.

The Scheduled-task pattern uses a scheduler, which is a component responsible for scheduling and executing tasks. The scheduler can be implemented using a variety of technologies, such as cron jobs, Windows Task Scheduler, or a custom scheduling system. The scheduler is responsible for determining when a task should be executed, and then triggering the task to run.

Tasks can be simple, such as sending an email or making an HTTP request, or complex, such as running a data processing pipeline. The scheduled-task pattern can be used to implement a variety of use cases, such as:

- Scheduling regular backups of databases and file systems
- Clearing old data from a system to save disk space
- Sending scheduled reports to users or customers
- Scheduling regular maintenance tasks, such as database optimization

- Scheduling regular updates to data feeds

Trade-offs:

- The scheduled-task pattern can add complexity to a system, as it requires additional components such as a scheduler and task management system.
- The scheduled-task pattern can also add overhead to a system, as tasks are executed at regular intervals, regardless of whether they are needed or not.
- The scheduled-task pattern can also cause issues with task coordination, if tasks are dependent on each other or have conflicting schedules.

Best Practices:

- Use a robust and well-tested scheduling system to avoid issues with task coordination and scheduling.
- Use a centralized task management system to ensure that tasks are executed on schedule and to track the progress of tasks.
- Monitor and test the scheduled tasks to ensure that they are working as expected and to detect and fix any issues.
- Use logging to track the execution of tasks and to diagnose issues.

Real-world examples:

- Apache Airflow is an open-source workflow management system that can be used to schedule and execute tasks.
- AWS Data Pipeline is a service that can be used to schedule and execute data-processing tasks on AWS.
- Quartz is an open-source job scheduling framework that can be used to schedule and execute tasks in Java-based systems.
- Apache Nifi is a data integration tool that can be used to schedule and execute data-processing tasks

Scheduler Agent Supervisor

Scheduler Agent Supervisor is a system design pattern that is used to manage the scheduling and execution of background tasks or processes in a distributed system. The pattern utilizes a supervisor or manager process that is responsible for monitoring the state of individual worker processes, and for starting and stopping them as needed.

The supervisor process can be implemented as a standalone service or as part of an existing service. It uses various techniques to monitor the state of the worker processes, such as sending heartbeat messages, checking status codes, or polling for status updates. The supervisor also uses a scheduling algorithm to determine when to start or stop worker processes based on factors such as resource usage, workload, or system capacity.

This pattern is commonly used in systems that require background processing of large amounts of data, such as data pipelines, batch processing jobs, or long-running tasks. Companies such as Google and Amazon use this pattern in their data processing and analytics systems to manage the execution of large-scale batch jobs and data processing tasks.

Trade-offs:

- It adds an additional layer of complexity to the system as it needs to manage and monitor the worker processes.
- It adds extra overhead for resource usage monitoring and scheduling.

Best Practices:

- Use a scheduling algorithm that can adapt to the changing workload and system conditions.
- Monitor the state of the worker processes regularly to ensure that they are running as expected.
- Use a supervisor service that can handle failures and recover from them gracefully.
- Use a supervisor service that can scale horizontally to handle large number of worker processes.

Real-world examples:

- Google's Borg and Kubernetes use this pattern to manage the execution of containerized workloads.
- Apache Mesos, an open-source cluster manager, uses this pattern to manage the execution of distributed applications.

- Amazon Elastic MapReduce (EMR), a managed big data platform, uses this pattern to manage the execution of data processing and analytics jobs.

Segregated Event Layers

The Segregated Event Layers pattern is a way of structuring the event-driven architecture of a system by separating the different types of events into different layers. This pattern allows for a more modular and flexible system design by allowing different parts of the system to handle different types of events without interfering with each other.

The pattern is based on the idea that events can be grouped into different layers based on their purpose and the part of the system that handles them. For example, there could be a layer for business events, which are events that are related to the core business logic of the system, and a layer for infrastructure events, which are events that are related to the underlying infrastructure of the system.

Each layer is handled by a separate component or service, and each layer is responsible for handling only the events that belong to it. This allows for a clear separation of concerns between the different parts of the system, and makes it easier to add or modify the handling of events.

The Segregated Event Layers pattern also allows for better scalability and performance by allowing different layers to be scaled independently. For example, the business event layer can be scaled to handle more events if the system is experiencing a high load, while the infrastructure event layer can be scaled to handle more events if the underlying infrastructure is experiencing a high load.

Trade-offs:

- It can be more complex to implement and maintain as there are more components and services to manage.
- It can be more difficult to ensure consistency across the different layers, and to handle events that span multiple layers.

Best Practices:

- Carefully plan the different layers and the events that belong to each layer.
- Implement clear interfaces between the different layers to ensure a clear separation of concerns.
- Monitor the performance and scalability of each layer and adjust as necessary.
- Keep the number of layers as small as possible to minimize complexity.

Real-world examples:

- Uber uses Segregated Event Layers pattern to separate the events related to their core business logic and the events related to their underlying infrastructure.
- Airbnb uses Segregated Event Layers pattern to separate the events related to their core business logic and the events related to their underlying infrastructure.

Segmented Log

The Segmented Log pattern is a way to manage a large, distributed log of events or messages in a distributed system. This pattern is typically used in systems that need to maintain a history of events or messages and allow for querying and processing of that history.

In a Segmented Log, the log is divided into smaller segments or partitions. Each segment is managed by a separate node or group of nodes in the system. This allows for more efficient management of the log, as each segment can be managed and replicated independently. The segments can also be distributed across different physical locations for added fault tolerance.

When a new event or message is added to the log, it is appended to the appropriate segment. The segments can be rotated or compacted over time to maintain a manageable size and improve performance.

This pattern is commonly used in systems such as databases, messaging systems, and event-driven systems. Companies such as Apache Kafka and Apache Cassandra use the Segmented Log pattern in their systems to manage large amounts of data.

Trade-offs:

- Segmenting the log can increase complexity in the system, as it introduces additional management and replication concerns.

- It may be more difficult to query and process the log when it is segmented, as data is spread across multiple segments.

Best Practices:

- Regularly rotate or compact the segments to maintain a manageable size and improve performance.

- Replicate each segment across multiple nodes for added fault tolerance.

- Use a Segmented Log library or tool that supports efficient management and querying of the log.

Real-world examples:

- Apache Kafka uses a Segmented Log pattern to manage the event streams in its distributed system.

- Apache Cassandra uses a Segmented Log pattern to manage the data in its distributed database.

- InfluxDB, a time series database, also uses a Segmented Log pattern.

Self-Healing Systems

Self-Healing Systems pattern is a system design pattern that focuses on the ability of a system to automatically detect and recover from failures, without the need for human intervention. This pattern can help prevent downtime and ensure the availability of a system, even in the event of failures.

Self-Healing Systems can detect failures through monitoring and monitoring tools that are built into the system. When a failure is detected, the system can automatically trigger a recovery process, such as restarting a failed service, or redirecting traffic to a backup server.

This pattern can be used in a variety of systems, such as distributed systems, cloud computing systems, and IoT systems. Companies such as Amazon and Google have implemented Self-Healing Systems in their cloud computing platforms to ensure high availability and minimize downtime.

Trade-offs:

- It can increase the complexity of the system, as it requires additional monitoring and recovery mechanisms to be implemented.

- It can also add extra latency to the system, as it may take some time for the system to detect and recover from failures.

Best Practices:

- Implement monitoring and monitoring tools to detect failures in the system.
- Test recovery mechanisms to ensure they work correctly.
- Use automation to trigger recovery processes, as it can reduce the time it takes to recover from a failure.
- Continuously monitor the system to detect and recover from new failures.

Real-world examples:

- Amazon's EC2 Auto Recovery feature automatically detects and recover from failures in Amazon's Elastic Compute Cloud (EC2) service.
- Google's SRE (Site Reliability Engineering) team uses self-healing systems in their cloud computing platform to minimize downtime.
- The Kubernetes container orchestration system has a built-in self-healing mechanism that automatically restarts failed containers.

Sequence Convoy

The Sequence Convoy pattern is a way to ensure that a specific sequence of events or actions occur in a distributed system. This pattern is often used in systems that need to maintain a specific order of operations, such as financial transactions or data replication.

In the Sequence Convoy pattern, a leader is chosen to coordinate the sequence of events. The leader is responsible for ensuring that each event in the sequence occurs in the correct order and that all participants in the system have completed their respective tasks before moving on to the next event.

For example, in a financial transaction system, the Sequence Convoy pattern could be used to ensure that a deposit is made before a withdrawal is allowed. The leader would coordinate the deposit and withdrawal operations to ensure that they occur in the correct order and that the deposit has been fully processed before allowing the withdrawal to proceed.

Trade-offs:

- It can add complexity to the system as it requires coordination between multiple components.

- It can also add latency to the system as it requires waiting for all components to complete their respective tasks before moving on to the next event.

Best Practices:

- Clearly define the sequence of events and the roles of each component in the system.
- Monitor the system to ensure that events are occurring in the correct order and that all components are completing their tasks.
- Use a leader election algorithm to ensure that the leader is always available and responsive.

Real-world examples:

- The Paxos algorithm, often used in distributed systems, is an example of the Sequence Convoy pattern.
- In database systems, the Sequence Convoy pattern is used to ensure that data replication occurs in the correct order and that all replicas have the same data.

- In distributed file systems, the Sequence Convoy pattern is used to ensure that changes to files are made in the correct order and that all replicas have the same data.

Service Decomposition

The Service Decomposition pattern is a method of breaking down a monolithic system into smaller, independent services that communicate with each other through APIs. This pattern allows for more flexibility and scalability in a system, as well as easier maintenance and deployment of individual services.

The Service Decomposition pattern involves identifying the core functionalities of the system, and breaking them down into separate services. Each service is then responsible for a specific set of functions, and communicates with other services through APIs. This allows for the system to be broken down into smaller, more manageable components, and also allows for services to be developed, deployed and scaled independently.

One of the key benefits of Service Decomposition is that it allows for the system to be more easily scaled, as services can be deployed on multiple servers or in the cloud. This also allows for easier maintenance and upgrades of individual services, without affecting the entire system.

Companies such as Amazon and Netflix have implemented the Service Decomposition pattern in their systems. Amazon uses service decomposition to break down their e-commerce platform into smaller services, such as the product catalog service and the order management service. Netflix uses service decomposition to break down their streaming platform into smaller services, such as the video streaming service and the user account service.

Trade-offs:

- It can be more complex to design and implement a system using the Service Decomposition pattern
- It can be more difficult to troubleshoot and debug issues when the system is composed of multiple services

Best Practices:

- Define clear boundaries for each service, and make sure that each service is responsible for a specific set of functionalities
- Design for loose coupling between services, so that changes to one service do not affect the others
- Implement a service registry to allow for easy discovery of services

Real-world examples:

- Amazon's e-commerce platform is composed of multiple services, such as the product catalog service and the order management service

- Netflix's streaming platform is composed of multiple services, such as the video streaming service and the user account service

Service Discovery

The Service Discovery pattern is a way to automatically discover the locations of services in a distributed system. This allows services to be located and accessed dynamically, without the need for hard-coded configurations or manual updates.

Service Discovery can be implemented using a variety of technologies, such as DNS, multicast DNS, and centralized service registries. In a centralized service registry, services register themselves with a central registry, and clients query the registry to locate a specific service. This can be beneficial in microservices architecture where there is a large number of services that need to be discovered.

Companies such as Netflix, Amazon and Google have implemented Service Discovery pattern to improve the scalability and resiliency of their distributed systems.

Trade-offs:

- It will add extra latency to the system as it will have to query the service registry before making a request.
- It will add extra complexity to the system as it will have to manage the service registry and the services registration.

Best Practices:

- Use a centralized service registry for high availability and scalability.
- Monitor the service registry for availability and responsiveness.
- Use a service discovery library that supports automatic service registration and deregistration.
- Use service discovery patterns in conjunction with load balancers for optimal performance.

Real-world examples:

- Netflix's Eureka and Amazon's AWS service discovery are examples of service discovery in action.
- Consul and Zookeeper are open-source service discovery tools that are widely used in the industry.
- Kubernetes, an open-source container orchestration platform, includes built-in service discovery via its Kubernetes Service resource.

Service Mesh

A service mesh is a configurable infrastructure layer for microservices application that makes communication between service instances flexible, reliable, and fast. It is responsible for traffic management, service discovery, load balancing, and security for service-to-service communication within a microservice architecture.

A service mesh typically consists of a data plane, which is responsible for handling the actual traffic, and a control plane, which is responsible for configuring and managing the data plane. The data plane is typically implemented as a set of proxies that are deployed alongside the service instances. These proxies intercept and handle all service-to-service communication, and can be configured to perform a variety of functions such as load balancing, traffic shaping, and service discovery.

The control plane is responsible for configuring the data plane proxies, and can be implemented using a variety of technologies such as Kubernetes, Istio, and Envoy.

Service mesh can be used in the different part of the system , such as traffic management: to control the flow of traffic between services, including routing and load balancing

Trade-offs:

- Service mesh can add complexity to the system and increase the number of moving parts.
- Service mesh can also add overhead to service-to-service communication in the form of additional network hops and processing.

Best Practices:

- Use service mesh in conjunction with other patterns such as circuit breaker and load balancing to provide a comprehensive set of features for service-to-service communication.
- Start with a minimal service mesh configuration and add features as needed.
- Monitor and troubleshoot service mesh using the built-in observability features.
- Use a service mesh that is native to the platform you are using, such as Istio for Kubernetes, to reduce the complexity of integrating the service mesh with your existing infrastructure.

Real-world examples:

- Istio is a popular open-source service mesh that can be used with Kubernetes.

- Linkerd is another popular open-source service mesh that can be used with any platform.

- Google's Cloud Load Balancing service provides a service mesh that can be used with Google Cloud Platform (GCP) services.

Service Registry

The Service Registry pattern is a way of discovering and connecting to services in a distributed system. The pattern involves maintaining a centralized registry of all available services and their locations. Clients can then use this registry to look up and connect to the appropriate service.

The Service Registry pattern is commonly used in microservice architectures, where there may be many services running on different machines and IP addresses. By maintaining a centralized registry, clients can easily discover and connect to the services they need, without having to hardcode IP addresses or ports.

One popular implementation of the Service Registry pattern is the use of a DNS service. A DNS service can be used to map service names to IP addresses and ports, allowing clients to easily discover and connect to services. Another popular implementation is the use of a service discovery tool such as Netflix Eureka, which is a service registry for distributed systems.

Trade-offs:

- A centralized service registry can become a bottleneck if it is not properly scaled.

- The registry can become a single point of failure in the system, so it's important to have a highly available and fault-tolerant registry.

Best practices:

- Design the registry to handle high traffic and scale horizontally.
- Implement monitoring and alerting to detect and respond to registry failures.
- Use a service discovery tool that supports service registration, discovery, and health checking.

Real-world examples:

- Netflix Eureka is a service registry used by Netflix to discover and connect to services in their distributed system.
- Consul and Zookeeper are other examples of service registry tools that are widely used in production systems.

Shared Data

The Shared Data pattern is used to handle shared data between multiple systems in a distributed system. This pattern involves the use of a centralized data store, such as a database, that can be accessed by multiple systems. This allows for consistent and efficient access to shared data, as well as the ability to easily update and maintain the data.

This pattern can be used in a variety of systems, such as distributed systems for large companies and financial institutions, for example, banks use shared data pattern for customer data, where multiple systems need to access the same customer data across different departments.

Trade-offs:

- The central data store can become a bottleneck if not properly scaled
- The data store can be a single point of failure if not properly implemented

Best Practices:

- Use a database that can handle high-concurrency read and write operations

- Implement proper indexing and caching to improve performance
- Use a data replication strategy to ensure data availability

Real-world examples:

- Amazon uses the shared data pattern in their e-commerce platform to store and access customer data across multiple systems
- Google uses the shared data pattern in their search engine to store and access web page data across multiple systems

Shared Nothing Architecture (SNA)

The Shared Nothing Architecture (SNA) is a distributed system design pattern in which each node in the system has its own local resources and does not share any memory or storage with other nodes. This allows each node to operate independently, without the need for locks or other synchronization mechanisms.

In a shared-nothing architecture, each node is responsible for managing its own data and processing tasks. This can be achieved through the use of partitioning, replication, or a combination of both.

Partitioning involves dividing the data and workloads among multiple nodes, so that each node is responsible for a specific subset of the data and workloads. Replication involves creating multiple copies of the data, so that each node has a complete copy of the data.

Shared Nothing Architecture is used in distributed databases, distributed caching and big data processing, such as Hadoop and Spark. Companies such as Facebook, Google and Amazon have implemented the shared-nothing architecture in their systems to improve scalability and performance.

Trade-offs:

- There is a potential for increased complexity when implementing the shared-nothing architecture, due to the need for partitioning and replication.
- It can also lead to increased network traffic, as nodes need to communicate with each other to access data.

Best Practices:

- Implementing proper partitioning and replication strategies can help minimize the trade-offs associated with the shared-nothing architecture.
- Monitoring the system's performance and adjusting the partitioning and replication strategies as necessary can help ensure optimal performance.

Real-world examples:

- Facebook's Cassandra NoSQL database uses the shared-nothing architecture.
- Google's Bigtable and Amazon's DynamoDB both use the shared-nothing architecture.
- Apache Hadoop and Apache Spark both use the shared-nothing architecture.

Shared State

Shared State is a design pattern that allows multiple parts of a distributed system to share a common state, without the need for locks or other synchronization mechanisms. This pattern is often used in systems that need to maintain a consistent view of a shared resource, such as a database or shared memory.

In a Shared State pattern, each node in the system has a copy of the shared state, and changes to the state are made by sending messages to other nodes. The nodes then update their copies of the state based on the messages they receive. This can be done using a variety of algorithms, such as Paxos or Raft, to ensure that the state is consistent across all nodes.

One of the key benefits of the Shared State pattern is that it allows for high availability and fault tolerance. If one node goes down, the other nodes can continue to operate and maintain the shared state. This can be useful in systems that need to maintain a consistent view of data, even in the presence of failures.

Companies such as Google and Facebook use the Shared State pattern in their distributed systems to ensure that data is consistent across all nodes.

Trade-offs:

- It can be challenging to ensure consistency across all nodes, especially in the presence of network partitions or other failures.

- The system can become complex and difficult to reason about as the number of nodes and shared state grows.

Best Practices:

- Use a consensus algorithm, such as Paxos or Raft, to ensure that the shared state is consistent across all nodes.

- Monitor the system to ensure that the shared state is being updated as expected and that there are no inconsistencies.

- Use tools such as distributed tracing to help understand how the system is behaving and identify potential issues.

Real-world examples:

- Google's Chubby is a shared state system that is used to coordinate updates to shared resources in distributed systems.

- Facebook's Cassandra is a distributed database that uses a shared state pattern to ensure consistency across all nodes.

- Apache Zookeeper is a distributed coordination service that uses a shared state pattern to manage configuration data and coordination across a cluster of machines.

Singular Update Queue

The Singular Update Queue pattern is used to ensure that updates to the shared resource are applied in the correct order and that there are no conflicts between updates. The queue is typically implemented as a lock-free data structure, such as a linked list, to minimize contention and improve performance.

When a thread or node wants to make an update to the shared resource, it places the update in the queue. A separate thread or process, known as the updater, is responsible for processing updates from the queue and applying them to the shared resource. The updater thread or process uses a lock or semaphore to ensure that updates are applied in the correct order and that there are no conflicts between updates.

The Singular Update Queue pattern can be useful for systems that need to manage updates to a shared resource in a multi-threaded or distributed environment, such as databases or in-memory caches. Companies such as Google and Facebook have used the Singular Update Queue pattern to improve the performance and scalability of their systems.

Trade-offs:

- It can add extra latency to the system as updates are queued and processed separately.
- It can add extra memory usage to the system as updates are stored in the queue.

Best Practices:

- Use a lock-free data structure, such as a linked list, to minimize contention and improve performance.
- Use a separate thread or process to process updates, known as the updater, so that updates can be applied in the correct order and that there are no conflicts between updates.
- Use a lock or semaphore to ensure that updates are applied in the correct order and that there are no conflicts between updates.

Real-world examples:

- Google's Bigtable and Spanner use Singular Update Queue pattern to manage updates.
- Facebook's Cassandra and Hbase use Singular Update Queue pattern to manage updates.

Single Socket Channel

Single Socket Channel is a system design pattern that is used to optimize the communication between a client and a server. In this pattern, a single socket connection is used for both sending and receiving data. This reduces the overhead of creating and managing multiple socket connections and can improve the performance of the system. Single Socket Channel is commonly used in high-performance systems that need to handle a large number of requests and responses in a short amount of time. Companies such as Google and Facebook have used this pattern in their systems to improve their network performance.

Trade-offs:

- It can lead to delays in processing requests if the channel becomes blocked.
- It may be difficult to scale the system as the number of requests increases.

Best Practices:

- Implement a message queue to handle incoming requests and outgoing responses.

- Monitor the socket connection to ensure that it is not blocked or overloaded.
- Implement flow control mechanisms to prevent overloading the channel.
- Use a library that supports non-blocking I/O and asynchronous operations.

Real-world examples:

- The Google Cloud Spanner database uses the Single Socket Channel pattern to optimize its network communication.
- The Facebook Messenger app uses the Single Socket Channel pattern for its real-time messaging feature.

Sidecar

The Sidecar pattern is a design pattern used in microservices architectures where a separate service is used to handle specific functionality for another service. The Sidecar service runs alongside the main service and communicates with it through a well-defined API. This separation of concerns allows for more flexibility in scaling, updating, and managing the services separately.

One example of the Sidecar pattern is using a service to handle security for another service. The main service handles the business logic and the Sidecar service handles the authentication and authorization for the main service. Another example is using a Sidecar service for handling service discovery for another service. The main service handles the business logic and the Sidecar service handles registering and discovering other services in the system.

Companies such as Netflix, Uber, and Google have implemented the Sidecar pattern in their microservices architectures to handle specific functionality and increase flexibility and scalability.

Trade-offs:

- Introduces an additional service and added complexity to the system
- Increases communication and coordination between services
- Adds extra latency to the system as it has to communicate with the sidecar service

Best Practices:

- Keep the sidecar service simple and focused on a specific functionality
- Use a well-defined API for communication between the main service and the sidecar service
- Monitor the sidecar service to ensure that it is working as expected
- Use a service discovery mechanism to automatically discover and register sidecar services

Real-world examples:

- Netflix's Zuul service is an example of a Sidecar service for handling API Gateway functionality for other services
- Istio, an open-source service mesh, uses a Sidecar service for handling service discovery and communication between services

- Kubernetes uses a Sidecar service for handling container logs and metrics for other services.

Space-based Architecture

The Space-based Architecture pattern is a way of designing distributed systems that utilizes a shared, centralized data store called a "space" to manage data and state. This pattern is based on the idea that all data and state should be stored in a single, globally accessible repository, rather than being distributed across multiple services or systems.

The Space-based Architecture pattern is often used in systems that require high scalability, availability, and performance. By centralizing data and state, the pattern can improve data consistency, reduce complexity, and simplify the management of distributed systems.

The Space-based Architecture pattern is often implemented using a distributed data grid or in-memory data grid (IMDG) technology. Companies such as Oracle, IBM, and GigaSpaces Technologies have developed products that implement the Space-based Architecture pattern.

Trade-offs:

- A centralized data store can be a bottleneck, and the system can become slow when the amount of data stored in the space becomes too large.

- A centralized data store can be a single point of failure, if the data store goes down the whole system goes down.

Best Practices:

- Design the Space-based Architecture pattern to be highly available and scalable.
- Ensure that the system can handle large amounts of data, and that data can be easily partitioned and distributed across multiple nodes.
- Monitor the space to ensure that it is operating efficiently, and that data is being properly distributed.

Real-world examples:

- Oracle Coherence is an example of a product that implements the Space-based Architecture pattern.
- GigaSpaces XAP is another example of a product that implements the Space-based Architecture pattern.
- IBM WebSphere eXtreme Scale is an example of a product that implements the Space-based Architecture pattern.

Shard/Sharding

Sharding is a technique for distributing a large dataset across multiple servers or machines. The goal of sharding is to improve the performance and scalability of a system by distributing the data and load across multiple servers. This allows for faster data retrieval and better handling of high traffic loads.

Sharding can be implemented in different ways, such as by partitioning the data based on a specific key, or by using a consistent hashing algorithm to distribute the data evenly across multiple servers.

One real-world example of sharding is used by companies like Facebook and Twitter, where they use sharding to distribute the large amount of data they collect from their users across multiple servers. This allows them to handle high traffic loads and improve the performance of their systems.

Trade-offs:

- Sharding can add complexity to the system, as it requires additional configuration and management of the data distribution.
- It may also require additional network communication between servers, which can add latency to the system.

Best Practices:

- Choose an appropriate sharding key that will distribute the data evenly across servers and minimize the number of hot spots.
- Use a sharding library that supports automatic data rebalancing and transparent data access.
- Monitor the system for performance bottlenecks and adjust the sharding configuration as needed.
- Use a consistent hashing algorithm to distribute data evenly across servers.

Real-world examples:

- Facebook uses sharding to distribute data from their users across multiple servers.
- Twitter also uses sharding to handle the large amounts of data they collect from their users.
- MongoDB, a popular NoSQL database, uses sharding to distribute data across multiple servers.

State Watch

The State Watch pattern is a system design pattern used in distributed systems to monitor the state of a particular resource or entity. The pattern involves creating a dedicated process or thread that continuously monitors the state of the resource and notifies other processes or threads when the state changes.

This pattern is commonly used in distributed systems where multiple processes or nodes need to be aware of the state of a particular resource, such as in distributed databases or distributed file systems. In these systems, the State Watch process can be used to monitor the state of the database or file system and notify other processes of any changes that occur.

The pattern can also be used in other types of distributed systems, such as cloud-based systems, where multiple instances of a service need to be aware of the state of a particular resource. In these systems, the State Watch process can be used to monitor the state of the resource and notify other instances of the service when the state changes.

Real-world examples:

- The ZooKeeper distributed coordination service, which is used by many distributed systems, uses the State Watch pattern to monitor the state of the system and notify clients of any changes that occur.

- Apache Cassandra, a distributed NoSQL database, uses the State Watch pattern to monitor the state of the system and notify clients of any changes that occur.

Trade-offs:

- The State Watch pattern requires a dedicated process or thread to continuously monitor the state of the resource, which can add additional overhead to the system.

- The pattern can also add additional latency to the system as other processes or threads need to wait for the State Watch process to notify them of changes to the resource.

Best Practices:

- Use a State Watch process or thread that is separate from the processes or threads that are using the resource.

- Use a State Watch process or thread that is able to handle multiple resources at the same time.

- Use a State Watch process or thread that can handle a high rate of change to the resource.

- Use a State Watch process or thread that can handle a high number of clients or subscribers.

Static Content Hosting

The Static Content Hosting pattern is used to offload the serving of static content, such as images, videos, and other media, to a separate service or group of services. This can help to improve the performance and scalability of the main application by reducing the load on its servers and allowing them to focus on serving dynamic content.

The static content is typically stored in a fast, highly available, and distributed storage system such as a Content Delivery Network (CDN) or object storage service. The main application then sends requests for static content to the separate service, which serves the content to the user.

This pattern can also be used to improve the security of the main application by reducing the attack surface and keeping sensitive data separate from public-facing content.

Companies such as Amazon, Google, and Akamai use CDN for their static content hosting.

Trade-offs:

- It will add extra latency as the request has to go through the separate service.

- It will add extra complexity as it requires maintaining and configuring a separate service.

Best Practices:

- Use a CDN service that has a large number of edge servers distributed globally to minimize the latency.
- Use a service that offers built-in security features such as SSL termination and DDoS protection.

Real-world examples:

- Amazon CloudFront is a popular CDN service used for static content hosting.
- Google Cloud CDN is another popular CDN service used for static content hosting.
- Akamai is a large CDN provider that offers static content hosting as a service.

Strangler Fig

The Strangler Fig pattern is a way of gradually introducing a new system while maintaining the existing one. The pattern is named after the fig tree, which starts as a seed in the branches of a host tree and gradually strangles it as it grows.

In this pattern, the new system is introduced alongside the existing system and is gradually given more and more responsibilities until it eventually takes over the entire system. This allows for a smooth transition without disrupting the current system or causing any downtime.

This pattern is often used in legacy systems, where it can be difficult or impossible to completely replace the existing system. Companies such as Netflix and Uber have used this pattern to gradually introduce new systems while maintaining their legacy systems.

Trade-offs:

- It can be a slow process, taking a longer time to fully introduce the new system.
- It can be more complex than a full-scale replacement.

Best Practices:

- Start by identifying the parts of the existing system that can be safely replaced.

- Focus on functionality that can be replicated before replacing the entire system.

- Use the existing system's interfaces to communicate between the new and legacy systems.

- Be prepared to rollback to the legacy system if necessary.

Real-world examples:

- Netflix's use of the Strangler Fig pattern to gradually replace their monolithic architecture with a microservices architecture.

- Uber's use of the Strangler Fig pattern to gradually replace their monolithic dispatch system with a microservices-based system.

Throttling

Throttling is a system design pattern that limits the rate at which a certain resource can be consumed. This pattern is used to prevent overuse of resources, such as CPU, memory, or network bandwidth.

The throttling pattern can be implemented in various ways, such as by using a token bucket or a leaky bucket algorithm. These algorithms are used to control the rate of requests by allowing a certain number of requests per time unit. If the number of requests exceeds the limit, the extra requests are rejected or delayed.

Throttling is often used in highly concurrent systems, such as web servers or cloud services, to prevent overloading the system and maintain a stable performance. For example, a web service may use throttling to limit the number of requests per second from a single IP address, to prevent a single client from overloading the server.

Companies such as Netflix and AWS use throttling to manage their services and improve the scalability of their systems.

Trade-offs:

- It can add extra latency to the system as it will have to check the state of the throttling before making a request.

- It can add extra memory usage to the system as it will have to keep track of the state of the throttling.

Best Practices:

- Monitor the system's performance to determine the appropriate throttling limit.

- Use a library that supports configurable rate limits and time windows.

- Use a consistent algorithm, such as token bucket or leaky bucket, across all resources.

Real-world examples:

- Netflix's Zuul API Gateway uses throttling to limit the number of requests from a single IP address.

- AWS's Elastic Load Balancer uses throttling to control the rate of incoming requests to a service.

- Apache Cassandra uses throttling to limit the number of requests to a single node.

Timestamp

The Timestamp pattern is used to provide a consistent ordering of events in a distributed system. Each event is assigned a unique timestamp, which can be used to order the events in the correct sequence.

In a distributed system, different nodes may generate events at different rates and these events may not arrive at a central location in the order they were generated. To ensure the correct ordering of events, each node assigns a unique timestamp to each event before it is sent to a central location for processing.

The timestamp can be generated using different techniques such as using a centralized time server, using a distributed time protocol like NTP or using a logical clock. The logical clock assigns timestamps based on the number of events generated by a node and the timestamps of events received from other nodes.

Timestamps are particularly useful in distributed systems that need to maintain an order of events, such as distributed databases and event-driven systems. Companies such as Google and Amazon use timestamping to maintain consistency and order in their distributed systems.

Trade-offs:

- The use of timestamps can add extra overhead to the system as each event needs to be assigned a timestamp
- In a system where there are large number of nodes, the process of ordering events based on timestamps can become complex and time-consuming

Best Practices:

- Use a centralized time server or a distributed time protocol to ensure that all nodes have a consistent view of time
- Use a logical clock to assign timestamps if a centralized time server is not available
- Use a timestamp format that can be easily compared and ordered such as Unix timestamps

Real-world examples:

- Google's Spanner database uses timestamps to maintain consistency in its globally distributed data
- Amazon's DynamoDB uses timestamps to maintain consistency in its distributed key-value store
- Apache Kafka uses timestamps to maintain the order of events in its distributed streaming platform.

Two Phase Commit (2PC)

Two Phase Commit (2PC) is a distributed algorithm that coordinates the commit or abort of a transaction across multiple systems.

The Two Phase Commit algorithm is used to ensure that a set of distributed transactions are either all committed or all rolled back. The algorithm is divided into two phases: the prepare phase and the commit phase.

In the prepare phase, each participant in the transaction votes either to commit or abort the transaction. If all participants vote to commit, the algorithm proceeds to the commit phase. If any participant votes to abort, the entire transaction is rolled back.

In the commit phase, the coordinator sends a commit message to all participants who have voted to commit. Each participant then commits the transaction locally.

Two Phase Commit is a widely used pattern in distributed systems, particularly in the context of databases. It is used to ensure that data is consistent across multiple systems, even in the case of failures. Companies such as Oracle and Microsoft SQL Server provide support for Two Phase Commit.

Trade-offs:

- 2PC is a synchronous protocol and requires all participants to be available and responsive for the duration of the protocol, which can add latency and increase the risk of blocking in case of failures.

- 2PC can add extra complexity to the system, as it requires additional messaging and coordination between participants.

Best Practices:

- Use Two Phase Commit only when necessary, as it can be overkill for many cases.

- Monitor the state of the Two Phase Commit protocol to ensure that it is running as expected and troubleshoot any issues that arise.

- Use a library or framework that provides support for Two Phase Commit, such as XA transactions.

Real-world examples:

- Oracle Database and Microsoft SQL Server provide support for Two Phase Commit as part of their distributed transaction support.

- Distributed systems such as Apache Kafka and RabbitMQ provide support for Two Phase Commit via their transaction APIs.

Version Vector

The Version Vector pattern is a method of maintaining consistency in a distributed system by keeping track of the version numbers of data items. Each data item in the system is assigned a unique version number, which is incremented each time the data item is updated. Each node in the system maintains a version vector, which is a mapping of version numbers to nodes. The version vector for a node contains the version numbers of all the data items that the node is aware of, along with the node ID of the node that last updated each data item.

When a node receives an update for a data item, it compares the version number in the update with the version number in its version vector. If the version number in the update is greater than the version number in the vector, the node accepts the update and increments its version vector for that data item. If the version number in the update is less than or equal to the version number in the vector, the node rejects the update as stale.

The Version Vector pattern can be used in distributed systems that need to maintain consistency and handle concurrent updates, such as distributed databases and file systems. Companies such as Google, Facebook and Amazon have implemented the Version

Vector pattern to improve the performance and consistency of their distributed systems.

Trade-offs:

- It can increase the complexity and overhead of the system as it needs to keep track of version numbers and version vectors for each node.
- It can also increase the communication overhead between nodes as each node needs to exchange version vectors with other nodes.

Best Practices:

- Use a unique and monotonically increasing version number for each data item.
- Maintain version vectors for each node in the system.
- Implement a mechanism to handle conflicts when two nodes have different version numbers for the same data item.
- Monitor the version vectors to ensure they are accurate and up-to-date.

Real-world examples:

- Google's Spanner distributed database uses the Version Vector pattern to maintain consistency across its global data centers.

- Facebook's Cassandra distributed database uses the Version Vector pattern to handle concurrent updates.

- Amazon's DynamoDB uses the Version Vector pattern to handle concurrent updates and maintain consistency in its distributed key-value store.

Versioned Value

The Versioned Value pattern is a method of maintaining consistency in distributed systems by assigning unique version numbers to each value. This pattern can be used to track updates to data and ensure that the most recent version is being used by all nodes in the system.

In a versioned value system, each value is assigned a version number, and all updates to the value must include the current version number. When a node receives an update, it checks the version number to ensure that it is the most recent version. If the version number is not the most recent, the update is rejected, and the node requests the current version from another node.

This pattern can be used in distributed systems to ensure that all nodes have the most recent version of a value and to prevent conflicts between updates from different nodes. For example, a distributed database system may use the Versioned Value pattern to ensure that all nodes have the most recent version of a record.

Trade-offs:

- It may introduce some additional network traffic as nodes are requesting the updated version of a value

- It may introduce extra complexity to the system as the version numbers have to be tracked and managed

Best Practices:

- Design the system to handle version conflicts and to ensure that the most recent version is always used.
- Monitor version numbers to detect conflicts and ensure that all nodes have the most recent version.
- Implement a mechanism for nodes to request the most recent version of a value.

Real-world examples:

- Google's Spanner database uses a versioned value system to ensure consistency across nodes.
- Amazon's DynamoDB uses a versioned value system to handle updates to data.
- Apache Cassandra uses a versioned value system to handle updates to data and ensure consistency across nodes.

Write-Ahead Log (WAL)

The Write-Ahead Log (WAL) pattern is a technique used in database systems to ensure data consistency and durability. This pattern involves writing all changes to the database to a log file before they are made to the actual database. This ensures that the changes are recorded in a durable manner and can be used to recover the database in case of a failure.

The WAL pattern works by keeping track of all changes made to the database in a log file. When a change is made, it is first written to the log file, and then applied to the actual database. If a failure occurs before the change is made to the actual database, the change can be recovered from the log file.

This pattern is commonly used in databases such as SQLite, PostgreSQL, and Oracle, and is particularly useful in systems that require high availability and data consistency. Companies such as Amazon, Google, and Facebook use the WAL pattern to ensure data durability and recoverability in their databases.

Trade-offs:

- WAL pattern increases the write time as it first writes the changes to the log file and then applies them to the actual database

- It also increases the disk space usage as it requires a separate log file to be maintained
- The system will be less performant as it needs to write to the log file before performing the actual write, which increases the time complexity.

Best practices:

- Regularly check and truncate the log file to ensure that it does not consume too much disk space.
- Keep a backup of the log file in case of disaster recovery.
- Monitor the state of the log file to ensure it is working as expected.

Real-world examples:

- SQLite uses the WAL pattern to ensure data durability and consistency
- PostgreSQL uses the WAL pattern to ensure data durability and consistency
- Oracle uses the WAL pattern to ensure data durability and consistency

www.ingramcontent.com/pod-product-compliance
Lightning Source LLC
LaVergne TN
LVHW041208050326
832903LV00021B/536